Palgrave Studies in Austrian Economics

This series provides insights to the key debates within Austrian economics. It presents advanced research that links current discussions on Austrian economics within its rich and influential intellectual tradition. Bringing together books from the leading researchers in this field, the varied the series aims to define the current scope of research within Austrian economics and shape directions of future analysis, with entries that offer both a foundation to the topic for those new to Austrian economics and fresh insights and debates for those who are well versed on the topic.

Roberta Adelaide Modugno

The Legacy of Murray N. Rothbard

Libertarian and Austrian Economist

palgrave
macmillan

Roberta Adelaide Modugno
Department of Political Science
Roma Tre University
Rome, Italy

ISSN 3005-0464 ISSN 3005-0472 (electronic)
Palgrave Studies in Austrian Economics
ISBN 978-3-032-06869-9 ISBN 978-3-032-06870-5 (eBook)
https://doi.org/10.1007/978-3-032-06870-5

Translation from the Italian language edition: "Murray N. Rothbard" by Roberta Adelaide Modugno, © IBL Libri 2022. Published by IBL Libri. All Rights Reserved.

This Palgrave Macmillan imprint is published by the registered company Springer Nature Switzerland AG
The registered company address is: Gewerbestrasse 11, 6330 Cham, Switzerland

To my father, Lino Modugno

Acknowledgments I would like to thank the Ludwig von Mises Institute for having generously allowed me to access and study the Rothbard Papers, preserved in their archives.

Competing Interests The author has no conflicts of interest to declare that are relevant to the content of this book.

Contents

About the Author

Roberta Adelaide Modugno is Professor of History of Political Thought at the Department of Political Science at Roma TRE University (Rome—Italy). Professor Modugno is fellow of the Ludwig von Mises Institute, where she has been often hosted as a Visiting Scholar. In August 2021 she received the International Prize Liberamente from Fondazione Scoppa and Confedilizia Calabria, for her contribution to the advancement of the values of freedom and classical liberalism. Professor Modugno participated to many conferences in Italy and abroad.

Among her main publications R. A. MODUGNO (Ed.), (Forthcoming). *Murray Rothbard on Politics, Philosophy and History. A Selection from his Papers*, Ludwig von Mises Institute; R. A. MODUGNO. (2022). *Murray N. Rothbard*, IBL Libri; R. A. MODUGNO (Ed.), (2009). *Murray N. Rothbard* versus *the Philosophers. Unpublished Writings on Hayek, Mises, Strauss and Polanyi*, Ludwig von Mises Institute; R. A. MODUGNO. (2019). The Libertarian Legacy of the Old Right: Democracy and Representative Government. *Journal of Libertarian Studies*, (23); R. A. MODUGNO. (2017). Liberty versus Democracy in Bruno Leoni and Friedrich von Hayek. *Libertarian Papers. A Journal of Philosophy, Politics and Economics*. 9 (2); R. A. MODUGNO. (2016). Liberalismo y democracia: un debate todavia abierto. In O. Iazzetta and M. R. Stabili (Eds.), *Las trasformaciones de la democracia. Miradas cruzadas entre Europa y América Latina*, Prometeo Libros, Buenos Aires.

CHAPTER 1

Introduction

Keywords Leviathan · libertarianism · Mises' seminar · politics · state

This book was first published in Italy by IBL Libri, in 2022.

A second English edition was necessary because of the importance that Rothbard's thought has for contemporary society and because of the changes that occurred in the world since 2022. Today, we are witnessing the growth and invasiveness of states, while in Europe, a supranational Leviathan has emerged, adding heavily to the oppression that individuals already suffer at the hands of their nation states. Rothbard's ideas are also particularly relevant today given the wars that are raging around the world.

Furthermore, in the United States, we are witnessing the dismantling of political correctness and woke ideology, which Rothbard already opposed in the 1990s. The election of Donald Trump seems to represent that kind of right-wing populism theorized and praised by Murray Rothbard. Finally, since 2023, another important novelty has emerged: the president of Argentina, Javier Milei, who is openly libertarian and a follower of Rothbard.

Why another book on Murray N. Rothbard, given there already exists a robust literature on Rothbard? Justine Raimondo, in *An Enemy on the State: the Life of Murray N. Rothbard,* published in 2000 (Raimondo, 2000), left to us an intellectual biography of Rothbard, David Gordon, in *The*

R. A. Modugno, *The Legacy of Murray N. Rothbard*, Palgrave Studies in Austrian Economics,
https://doi.org/10.1007/978-3-032-06870-5_1

Essential Rothbard, published in 2007 (Gordon, 2007), gives a broad overview of Murray N. Rothbard's thought and work and shows how intertwined are Rothbard's libertarianism and Austrian economics. Gerard Casey, in *Murray Rothbard*, published in 2010 (Casey, 2010), concentrates primarily on making the case for free market anarchism. The main core of this book is Rothbard's libertarianism. So, again, why another book on Rothbard? I think it is needed to provide an analytical and critical study putting together his economics and political philosophy. The present book gives new insights into the existing studies in the field. It includes previously unpublished Rothbard material that had been conserved by the Mises Institute and has been lent to me for publishing. From this, I made several important discoveries, key to our understanding of the development of his thought: the search for a rational foundation of ethics; his interest in anarcho-capitalism; his criticism of democracy; and the origins of the Austrian school of economics.

I approached this topic using the methodology of the history of political thought. This kind of perspective gives great importance to the historical events, shaping Rothbard's ideas and the political discourse of the times. Lastly, the author's cultural legacy is examined. Considering all this, it seemed appropriate to make it available to the English-speaking public.

My personal interest on Murray Newton Rothbard began in the late summer of 1995. While locked up in the beautiful Firestone Library at Princeton University, where I was to study the American feminist movement of the nineteenth century, I found myself devouring *For a New Liberty: The Libertarian Manifesto* (Rothbard, 1973) and *The Ethics of Liberty* (Rothbard, 1982). Before my departure to the United States, my professor Dario Antiseri suggested that I read Karen Vaughn's book *Austrian Economics in America: The Migration of a Tradition* (Vaughn, 1994). Professor Antiseri told me that in that book I would find the names of scholars who, in the 1950s and 1960s, had attended Ludwig von Mises's famous seminar on Austrian economics at New York University. I did, but I was particularly intrigued by Vaughn's references to Rothbard, who seemed to me so brilliant and bizarre at the same time. I decided I should get to know Rothbard by reading his texts. It was through Vaughn's book that I discovered that there were professors who followed and knew Rothbard teaching at New York University.

One morning I took the train to New York, enthusiastic about trying to find a way to meet Rothbard at NYU. Arriving there, I was greeted with great courtesy by professors Israel Kirzner and Mario Rizzo. The latter informed me, with deep sadness, that Rothbard had unfortunately passed away prematurely in January 1995. Perhaps sympathizing with me, Mario Rizzo invited me to attend the Mises seminar that same afternoon. All this not only changed my academic life, which was just beginning, but changed my way of perceiving the market, the economy, society, and above all the state. Ultimately, the intellectual encounter with Rothbard and his cultural surroundings changed my vision of the world. I came from a family in which merit was held in high regard. Since I was a child, my mother had told me the parable of the talents over and over again! And my father, a classical liberal, told me that if you want to help a person in need, it is better to teach him to fish than to give him fish!

Besides these personal memories, Rothbard helped me see politics from a different perspective, and I realized that many things we all take for granted—such as the state, the idea of homeland, society, war, and national borders—should not at all be taken for granted: they are often the results of habits, customs, and education. The state is by no means the only possible political synthesis for the solution of the political problem—that is to say, the problem of power, why some men obey others. The state is one of the political syntheses that human inventiveness has created to resolve the question of civil and peaceful coexistence. Is this the only possible solution? Has it always existed? Does it solve the problem of what is the best regime? Moreover, does it even make sense to ask the question of what is the best regime? Has the state really managed to protect the natural rights of individuals, life, freedom, property, and the pursuit of happiness? Or is the reality of the state something different? Anyone who has the desire and curiosity to ask these questions will find in Rothbard an ally and a friend who will ideally take him by the hand and accompany him through an exciting but sometimes bitter adventure.

References

Casey, G. (2010). *Murray Rothbard*. Bloomsbury.

Gordon, D. (2007). *The essential Rothbard*. Ludwig von Mises Institute.

Raimondo, J. (2000). *An enemy of the state: The life of Murray N. Rothbard*. Prometheus.

Rothbard, M. N. (1973). *For a new liberty: The libertarian manifesto*. Macmillan.

Rothbard, M. N. (1982). *The ethics of liberty*. New York University Press.

Vaughn, K. (1994). *Austrian economics in America: The migration of a tradition*. Cambridge University Press.

CHAPTER 2

Biography and Historical and Cultural Context

Keywords Old right · Education · Classical liberalism · Austrian school · Libertarianism · Objectivism · Cold war

1 Biographical Profile and Education

Murray Newton Rothbard (see Block & Rockwell, 1988; Bassani, 1996, 2004; Modugno, 1998, 2009, forthcoming; Rockwell, 1995; Hoppe, 1998; Raimondo, 2000; Gordon, 2007; Casey, 2010; Marcognat, 2012; Iannello, 2017) was born in the Bronx in New York City on March 2, 1926, to Jewish parents, immigrants from Poland determined to enter American society. Rothbard's father, David, was born near Warsaw and emigrated in 1910. A chemist in the oil industry, David Rothbard, was a staunch individualist, believing in rationality and science. Father and son strongly believed in the ideals of freedom and individualism, but they found themselves surrounded by a large group of relatives of socialist orientation, with whom they engaged in heated discussions. The two were very close, and David Rothbard played a crucial role both as a source of ideological inspiration and as a moral support for his son. Young Murray was a lively and intelligent child with a strong personality, and during elementary school he already showed a certain impatience with public school and its attempts to force him to conform to things he did

R. A. Modugno, *The Legacy of Murray N. Rothbard*, Palgrave Studies in Austrian Economics,
https://doi.org/10.1007/978-3-032-06870-5_2

not intend to conform to. As a result, David and Raya Rothbard opted for a good private school, albeit with some financial sacrifice (Raimondo, 2000; Rockwell, 1995).

Rothbard grew up in an environment of intense political debate and soon found himself criticizing Roosevelt's New Deal. "I grew up in a communist culture; the middle-class Jews in New York whom I lived among, whether family, friends, or neighbors, were either communists or fellow-travelers in the communist orbit. I had two sets of Communist Party uncles and aunts, on both sides of my family" (Rothbard, 1994, 4). Rothbard's love of freedom developed very early, as did his aversion to the egalitarianism he experienced in public schools. By the end of high school, young Murray's thinking was already characterized by a strong opposition to communism, New Deal policies, and militarism. These positions led Rothbard to approach the major players of the Old Right (see Nash, 1976; Rothbard, 2007; Raimondo, 2014; Modugno, 2019, pp. 5–21)—Albert Jay Nock, Henry Louis Mencken, Frank Chodorov, Rose Wilder Lane, and Senator Robert Taft—that is, that group of libertarian intellectuals opposed to the New Deal, prohibitionist policies, any intervention of the United States in foreign policy, and any form of economic interventionism and collectivism in domestic politics. Hostile to the spread of Roosevelt statism in domestic politics, the movement subsequently, at the end of the 1930s, strenuously opposed the drift of global military interventionism on the foreign policy side. "Since the essence of the Old Right was a reaction against runaway Big Government at home and overseas," Rothbard writes, "the Old Right was necessarily, even if not always consciously, libertarian rather than statist, 'radical' rather than traditional conservative apologists for the existing order" (Rothbard, 2007, p. 2). To understand the essence of this movement, it is necessary to seek its roots in that dramatic event that was the First World War.

The war was especially traumatic for anyone who had been opposed to the entry of the United States. The total mobilization, repression of opponents, carnage, and global intervention of the United States on an unprecedented scale led to strong reactions from many people. The polarization of public opinion did not cease with the end of the conflict. The war, with its corollary of repression and militarization, started a critical rethinking of the American system itself. In addition, the international balance that emerged from the conflict was crystallized and became the norm in the postwar era. The Treaty of Versailles and the League of Nations meant that America could not forget the war and simply leave it behind. Those who had opposed the conflict were joined by former supporters of President Wilson who were disillusioned with the reality of the world he had created. The various oppositions, pre- and postwar, united themselves in a coalition that included socialists, progressives, and individualists. All of them were clearly anti-militarist and unpatriotic, embracing radical anti-statism. Although the Socialist Party split and lost its relevance during the postwar era, the individualist component of the opposition grew substantially during the 1920s. Part of that opposition was not only political but cultural, a revolt against those retrograde and Victorian customs that characterized American society. Part of this revolt was represented by the well-known "lost generation" of young American writers who expressed their intense disenchantment with wartime idealism and their recognition of the harsh reality that militarism and war had revealed about America. A cultural aspect of this revolt and disillusionment was the advent of the jazz era, with its search for social and cultural freedom in the yearning for individual expression.

In 1942, Rothbard entered Columbia University, his poor eyesight having spared him from the draft. Socially and politically, he found himself rather isolated. He was, in fact, a young man of the Old Right—that is, of that generation of men and women before him who represented conservatives, classical liberals, and libertarians—supporters of the narrow movement called America First, which was outlawed when the United States entered the Second World War. The ideological climate at Columbia University was oriented toward leftist ideas. The United States and the Soviet Union were united in the struggle against Nazi and fascist enemies; as a result, free market values were not considered central to the political discussion. With the end of the war, Rothbard renewed his hopes that the principles of classical liberalism—that is, the ideals of the nineteenth century: economic freedom and the minimal state—could triumph, and he joined the New York Young Republican Club with the aim of promoting free market ideas.

In 1946, George Stigler, who would win the Nobel Prize in 1982 but at the time was still a young professor of economics, began teaching at Columbia University. The young Rothbard was fascinated by his personality and teachings. In his early lectures, Stigler criticized rent control policy and introduced the idea that the minimum wage did nothing but harm workers and exclude many from the labor market. Rothbard immediately wrote to the Foundation for Economic Education for a copy of Stigler and Milton Friedman's work *Roof or Ceiling*? (Friedman, 1946)

Rothbard thus came into contact with the libertarian movement for the first time. With the end of the Second World War, free market and limited government principles seemed out of fashion. In fact, the end of the conflict had brought Americans the expansion of state power, a partially controlled economy, millions of conscripts, more taxes, and increased public spending. In short, the old classical liberalism now seemed outdated, but it was not at all dead and would soon experience an unexpected revival. In the Foundation for Economic Education, Rothbard discovered that the classical libertarian and liberal principles of the Old Right were not dead but that, in the shadows, during the darkest years, a new generation of liberals was preserving this glorious tradition. The Foundation for Economic Education was founded in 1946 by Leonard Read precisely for the promotion and advancement of studies in the field of libertarian thought. It was based in a building in Irvington-on-Hudson, close to New York City, and it gathered young libertarian economists. In addition to publishing books and pamphlets, it had its own scientific journal, *Freeman*.

Also in 1946, Rothbard received his master's degree in economics and mathematics, and in 1948 he was admitted to the PhD course in economics under the guidance of Professor Joseph Dorfman. In this same period, there was an important novelty in Rothbard's life: he met a girl who was strolling through Columbia's campus—JoAnn Schumacher. The two soon became inseparable, and Joey, as Murray called her, became his lifelong companion. For Rothbard, Joey was "the indispensable frame" of his life and work. After graduating with a bachelor's degree in history from Columbia, JoAnn Schumacher continued her master's degree at New York University. She had a great passion for classical music, and in particular for opera, which she shared with Murray. The two married in 1953 but had no children. Joey dedicated her whole life to her husband, supporting him and helping him in his work. In 1956, Rothbard defended his doctoral thesis, "The Panic of 1819: Reactions and Policies," and earned his PhD in economics. The work was published in 1962 (Rothbard, 1962).

Liberal individualism was still alive in the United States, and among the leading figures of the new generation of activists who played an important role in the formation of the young Rothbard was Frank Chodorov (1887–1966). Already in 1944, he began publishing the monthly magazine *analysis*, which ran for six years and managed to keep alive the libertarianism of the Old Right. Chodorov addressed issues such as income tax, public schools, protectionism, and various iconic themes of statism. In 1947, Chodorov opened a bookstore, Analysis, which offered fundamental texts of the American libertarian tradition. Opposition to the state's subsidization of business and to the Cold War became central to the debate that grew in the emerging libertarian movement. It was largely thanks to Chodorov's bookstore that Rothbard cultivated his own ideas, reading authors such as Lysander Spooner, Benjamin Tucker, Auberon Herbert, Albert Jay Nock, Henry Louis Mencken, Garet Garret, Rose Wilder Lane, and Isabel Paterson. Rothbard was also impressed by Chodorov's *Taxation Is Robbery* and began to collaborate with both *analysis* and *Freeman*, a magazine directed by Henry Hazlitt. It was in this way that Rothbard came into contact with the great libertarian tradition, but his anarchocapitalist position had already matured during his university days. As Rothbard himself recalls, one evening in the winter of 1949–1950, during a conversation with some left-wing students, he realized that it was a blatant contradiction to be in favor of the free market and at the same time to admit violent government actions such as taxation, war, and the interference of the state in the lives of citizens. He concluded, "My whole position was inconsistent ... there were only two logical possibilities: socialism, or anarchism. Since it was out of the question for me to become a socialist, I found myself pushed by the irresistible logic of the case, a private property anarchist, or, as I would later dub it, an anarcho-capitalist" (Rothbard, 1988, p. 53). Obviously, Rothbard opted for an individualistic and free market anarchism based on the logical extension of laissez-faire. At this point, having the New York Public Library at his disposal, he devoured the writings of individualist anarchists of the American tradition, such as Benjamin Tucker and Lysander Spooner.

A pivotal moment in Rothbard's education was his encounter with Ludwig von Mises (1881–1973) and the ideas of the Austrian school of economics. Due to the occupation of Austria by Nazi Germany, many of the members of the Austrian school emigrated to the United States. Among them was Mises, whose personal library had been burned by the Nazis. When Mises arrived in the United States, he was already almost 60, was not particularly fluent in English, and lacked an official academic position. The Volker Fund then funded a seminar on the Austrian school of economics, which Mises held at New York University from 1949 until shortly before his death. Among the fundamental ideas of the Austrian school are methodological individualism, the subjective versus the labor theory of value, diminishing marginal value, spontaneous order, the evolutionary theory of political and social institutions, the a priori approach to human action, the impossibility of economic calculation in a planned economy, the free market, and the preeminence of deductive logic over mathematics in economic science. Mises's seminar was a pivotal event in the American cultural context and the cornerstone of what has been called the migration of Austrian ideas to America (Vaughn, 1994). It was precisely this intellectual migration that was the source of the rebirth of classical liberalism in the United States, where the individualistic political tradition experienced a revitalization but also a radicalization, developing in several directions, the Chicago school being one example. In Rothbard's case, the encounter with Mises and the discovery of the Austrian school were the backbone of his intellectual formation, serving as a bridge between his passion for the classical American liberal tradition and a pure free market economic theory. Rothbard was thus able to combine an ethical tradition founded on the natural law of the founding fathers and John Locke with the Austrian tradition, in which the concept of natural law was absent. The result was a very original thought that deeply reshaped the Austrian school of Carl Menger (1840–1921), Mises, and Friedrich von Hayek (1899–1992), as will be explored later.

While attending Mises's seminar, Rothbard met young students who learned to love Mises and were deeply influenced by the legacy of the Old Right, which he continued to view as central to his education. These students, as Justin Raimondo recalls, saw in Rothbard a point of reference, and the experience gave life to an informal group, the Circle Bastiat. In addition to Rothbard and his wife, Joey, it included Leonard Liggio, who was a sophomore in high school, Ralph Raico, George Reisman, and Ronald Hamowy. All of them were destined for a bright future in academic life and as libertarian scholars. But at the time, they were a cheerful company who gathered, argued passionately, played board games, and composed their songs (Raimondo, 2000, p. 82). Rothbard increasingly became a point of reference for sympathizers of libertarian ideas and supporters of Austrian school economics. The Rothbards' apartment on the Upper West Side of Manhattan became a meeting point for scholars, future philosophers, politicians, professors, and students.

Around the mid-1950s, Rothbard attended the "objectivist" group of Ayn Rand (1905–1982), who fled the Soviet Union in 1926 and supported capitalism as the only means of human fulfillment. The Randian movement spread above all among young American university students who were attracted by her rationalism and unhappy with what was becoming the conservatism of the New Right. Rand, after fleeing the Soviet Union, produced her entire literary and philosophical output in the United States, including the famous dystopian novel *Anthem* (Rand, 1938) and *The Fountainhead* (Rand, 1994). Rand and her followers met every Saturday night in her living room and read pages of her later writings. Her thought and strong personality translated into a real cult, marked at times by aspects of fanaticism. Relations between Rand and her followers were not, therefore, always calm and idyllic. Noteworthy is the story of the quarrel between Rand and Rothbard caused by the fact that the latter's wife devoted herself to charity, because of which Rand insisted that Murray exchange her for another wife (Tuccille, 1971, pp. 21–24). Of course, relations between Rand and Rothbard soon broke down.

Meanwhile, major changes were taking place in American political culture. By the mid-1950s, the first generation of the Old Right was nearing its end. Not only was the Old Right less numerous and influential than in the 1930s and 1940s but with the advent of the Cold War it was abandoning its traditional anti-imperialist and anti-militarist position. Rothbard, therefore, began a very difficult period, unable to share the position of the conservative "cold warriors." He launched his attack against the Cold War in the pages of a periodical called *Faith and Freedom*. Rothbard, for whom it was inconsistent to accept militarism, did not spare the new exponents of the right from criticism, reproaching them for having lost their role as supporters of peace by becoming militarists and interventionists. In the era of the arms race, Rothbard called for disarmament. All this made him unpopular within the Right itself, and his signature disappeared from *Faith and Freedom*. William Buckley, in 1955, had founded the *National Review*, which became the reference point for the American Right. Rothbard collaborated with the magazine for five years, becoming an active part of its intellectual circle, writing articles, reviews, and participating in events organized by Buckley. The Cold War and the struggle against the Soviet Union became the main cause of the *National Review*, for which even the containment of public spending, state functions, and the tax burden could be sacrificed. The same fate befell Rothbard as his position became increasingly critical toward the interventionist position against communism—a position supported by Buckley himself. At this point, in the middle of the Cold War, Rothbard was a victim of the purge conducted by Buckley at the magazine and found himself politically isolated. In 1960, he broke ties with the Right to follow his consistent anti-militarist stance. Rothbard, in the first half of the 1960s, began to focus on the Leviathan state as the enemy—the alliance between big government and big business to the detriment of an exploited middle class—as well as the entire military industrial complex. The old alliance between conservatism and libertarianism had failed. David Gordon deepened this point in his book *The Essential Rothbard*, referring to an essay written by Rothbard for the *National Review* in April 1959 and never published by the magazine. This is what Gordon defines a "devastating objection": "In all the reams of material written by the Right in the last decade [1949–1959], there is never any precise spelling-out of what a policy of ultrafirmness or toughness really entails. Let us then fill in this gap by considering what I am sure is the *toughest possible* policy: an immediate ultimatum to Khrushchev and Co. to resign and disband the whole Communist regime; otherwise we drop the H-bomb on the Kremlin … . What is wrong with this policy? Simply that it would quickly precipitate an H-bomb, bacteriological, chemical, global war which would destroy the United States as well as Russia" (Gordon, 2007, p. 95; 2010). As Gordon explains, according to Rothbard, defeating Russia would lead to "national suicide," the destruction of the United States and the only alternative is the return to the American traditional neutrality. This means pursuing a foreign policy supporting a program of world disarmament. "Mutual disarmament—Gordon writes—was in Russia's interest as well, so a disarmament agreement was entirely feasible." The world trade would benefit from this and Russia itself (Gordon, 2007, p. 96).

In 1966, Rothbard began teaching at the Polytechnic Institute of Brooklyn, where he remained until 1986. Teaching allowed him to devote himself to studying and writing with a certain degree of economic security. The 1960s marked for Rothbard the rise of the New Left youth movement and the creation of an independent libertarian movement. By 1965, the welfare-warfare state was growing dramatically, and Rothbard participated in the protest movement against the Vietnam War in a climate of mounting tension. With the left-wing youth, he shared criticism of the military–industrial complex and its links with the state. Rothbard, always looking for new alliances, joined in 1968 the Peace and Freedom Party, an emanation of the youth protest movement. In this period, he found himself in an environment decidedly uncongenial to him: he was surrounded by hippies, left-wing anarchists, and Trotskyists. But he always stayed true to his principles and never abandoned his devotion to the free market and private property. In 1965, Rothbard and Leonard Liggio (1933–2014) founded the periodical *Left and Right.*

On the Republican side, in 1969, at the meeting of the youth organization, Young Americans for Freedom in St. Louis, there was a break between the libertarians and the rest of the movement. The conflict again focused on the Vietnam War and conscription, which libertarians strenuously opposed. On that occasion, a draft card was publicly burned. The break was inevitable, and an independent libertarian movement was born. The Society for Individual Liberty operated on the East Coast, and the California Libertarian Alliance on the West Coast. From these movements, the Libertarian Party was born in 1972, and Rothbard joined in 1973.

In the early 1970s, Rothbard was invited by multibillionaire Charles Koch (1935–2021) to spend a weekend at his cottage in the mountains of Colorado. The purpose was to discuss the future libertarian movement, and from this meeting, the Cato Institute was born, which in 1977 established its headquarters in San Francisco, the city that was also the headquarters of the Libertarian Party. The creation of a libertarian think tank seemed to be the realization of Rothbard's dream. The Rothbardian strategy was, in fact, focused on the idea of the need for the dissemination of libertarian ideas, the training of young libertarian scholars, and the creation of intellectual figures of reference. The Cato Institute founded the *Journal of Libertarian Studies.* It organized conferences, seminars, and academic programs. During the beginning of the 1980s, however, the environment at the Cato Institute began to deteriorate. Clashes between different factions and personalities undermined the institute's serene atmosphere. In particular, there were disagreements between Rothbard and Ed Crane—Koch's representative—about Rothbard's approach, which was decidedly too radical. The Cato Institute moved to Washington, D.C., to become the first conservative think tank. Rothbard, having abandoned the Cato Institute, took another path, returning to his roots in the Old Right.

In 1982, at the behest of Llewellyn H. Rockwell, Margit von Mises (Mises's widow), and Rothbard, the Ludwig von Mises Institute was founded in Auburn, Alabama, and Rothbard accepted the position of vice president for academic affairs. The *Review of Austrian Economics* was founded under Rothbard's direction. The institute's academic programs and summer seminars began to attract the attention of students and scholars from all over the United States but also from abroad. Students were fascinated by Rothbard's monumental culture and humor. The Mises Institute allowed him free and full intellectual expression, and his association with Rockwell lasted until Rothbard's untimely death.

With the fall of the Berlin Wall in 1989 and the implosion of communist regimes, the Old Right reappeared on the ideological political scene. With the end of the Cold War, at least part of the conservative movement, gathered around the Mises Institute, gave clear signs of wanting to recover its anti-interventionist tradition. Rothbard, in some way ideally, came back home, reestablishing his association with the conservative Right. He and Rockwell founded the *Rothbard–Rockwell Report,* and in 1985, the Mises Institute began publishing the magazine *Free Market*. Rothbard sided against the first Gulf War, considering it an unjust war, and against NAFTA (the North American Free Trade Agreement), considering it a form of mercantilism.

This was a particularly happy time for Murray. In 1985, he was appointed S. J. Hall Distinguished Professor of Economics at the University of Nevada in Las Vegas, although he and Joey periodically traveled to their beloved New York to attend opera performances. This academic recognition gave him new energy, and he witnessed with great satisfaction the spread of the ideas of the Austrian school and libertarianism. Unfortunately, however, he did not have much time left to live. He died suddenly in New York on January 7, 1995.

Here is how Llewellyn Rockwell remembered him: "In his work, as in his life, he always sided with the pro-liberty forces against the welfare-warfare. He especially liked the anti-New Dealers, the anti-imperialists, the Confederates, the anti-federalists, the tax resisters, the underground businessmen, the anti-state pamphleteers, and other unsung heroes. Throughout history, the power elite has found profitable uses for the state. Rothbard never passed up a chance to name them, to explain how they did it, and to show how their actions harmed everyone else in society" (Rockwell, 1995, p. 110).

2 Historical and Cultural Context

No political theory is detached from its historical and cultural context. Rothbardian thought unfolds through crucial moments in the history of the twentieth century, accompanied by a cultural climate and equally significant currents of thought. It is Rothbard himself who reveals to us what became his cultural context of reference—namely the Old Right—in a work published posthumously but which is fundamental to understanding the genesis and evolution of Rothbardian thought: *The Betrayal of the American Right* (Rothbard, 2007). The Old Right had as its main points of reference Albert Jay Nock and Henry Louis Mencken. They inspired Garet Garrett, Frank Chodorov, Isabel Paterson, Rose Wilder Lane, John T. Flynn, Senator Robert Taft, and Chicago Tribune editor Robert McCormick. On the whole, the movement opposed Roosevelt's New Deal policies and interventionist military policy abroad. In general terms, those who identified with the culture of the Old Right wanted the restoration of the classical liberalism of the founding fathers and a government whose purpose was strictly limited to defending the right to private property. Specifically, opposition to New Deal policies meant calling for the abolition of the entire welfare state, the Wagner Act, the Social Security Act, and the measure by which Congress on June 5, 1933, abolished the gold standard in the United States following the crisis of 1929. Later, belonging to the Old Right meant opposing America's entry into the Second World War and Woodrow Wilson's entire foreign policy—that is, the idea of making the United States the guardian of the world and promoter of democracy. Others opposed the entire Federal Reserve System, and still others, including Rothbard himself, wanted the restoration of the dear old Articles of Confederation, which represented the first American constitution up to the Philadelphia Convention (Rothbard, 2000, p. 4).

During the Second World War, the Old Right lived its darkest days. Libertarians and isolationists were vilified, assaulted, and persecuted until they disappeared from the ideological spectrum. But as America emerged from the war effort, a new generation of libertarians tied to the old tradition was emerging. They believed in laissez-faire and nonintervention in foreign policy. Senator Robert Taft, a leading figure for the Old Right, was very skeptical of the Truman Doctrine, opposed the Marshall Plan and the creation of NATO, and engaged in the challenge against the Cold War. With the rejection of the Bricker Amendment[1] and the disappearance of Robert Taft and Robert McCormick, it seemed that the old tradition was doomed. The end of the war had meant the enlargement of the state, a partially controlled economy, millions of conscripts, more taxes, and more

[1] In 1951, Republican Senator John W. Bricker proposed an amendment to preserve the discretionary authority of Congress over the incorporation of international law into American law. The Eisenhower administration rejected it.

public spending. In those years, however, a new intellectual climate, favorable to the rebirth of classical liberalism, took shape. The publication of *Human Action* (Mises, 1998), *Bureaucracy* (Mises, 1944a), and *Omnipotent Government* (Mises, 1944b) by Ludwig von Mises and *Road to Serfdom* (Hayek, 1944) by Friedrich von Hayek helped to create a decidedly more open environment for individualism and ideas in favor of the free market, which paved the way for the resurgence of liberalism. In 1944, Mises published *Omnipotent Government* and *Bureaucracy*, to which classical liberals and American libertarians owe an enormous intellectual debt. *Bureaucracy* is a brilliant analysis of bureaucracy and the profound difference between profit-oriented and state and bureaucratic management. *Omnipotent Government* points out that the German Nazi state was in essence nothing more than a variant of socialism and collectivism. When Hayek's *Road to Serfdom* came out in 1944, the work had a shocking effect in American and British intellectual circles. Dedicated to socialists of all parties, the work revolves around the thesis that planning and socialism are incompatible with freedom, the rule of law, and democracy. Nazi and fascist regimes are presented as aspects of collectivism. The social democracy of the Weimar Republic was nothing but the embryo of Nazism. Economic planning, Hayek warns, necessarily leads to the suppression of freedom, all-encompassing control, and totalitarianism.

Nazism and fascism were not reactions against socialism at all but the product of the socialist tendencies of the previous period. He warns of the dangers of abandoning the path of individualism and liberalism and taking the path of slavery—the path chosen by Germany and Italy, which was becoming dangerously popular in England and the United States. Hayek contrasts this spectrum with the abandoned path of individualism and classical liberalism. Hayek's work was a huge and unexpected success in America, and its reception was fundamental to the revival of liberalism. As George Nash notes, the interventionist policies of the New Deal were still an important matter for Americans, because their triumph and the consensus granted by the population were still uncertain. Hayek's work appeared as a polemical and competent challenge. The remaining libertarians and classical liberals of the Old Right could not but rejoice when such vigorous support for their ideas appeared. "An old tradition had acquired an articulate voice again .... Hayek *was* on their side .... At last they had a champion who made the enemy squirm" (Nash, 1976, p. 7). In 1953, Erik von Kuehnelt-Leddihn hailed the "resurrection" of liberalism (Kuehnelt-Leddihn, 1953, pp. 337–339).

As Nash notes, books alone were not enough to create an intellectual movement that could also have political implications (Nash, 1976, p. 17). Organizations were needed to gather those who recognized themselves in common ideas. In 1946, Leonard Read established the Foundation for Economic Education in Irvington-on-Hudson, New York, supported by classical liberals such as Mises and Hayek. Leonard Read was convinced that the main problem to overcome was illiteracy in economics, so he undertook the mission of educating Americans in this area. In 1947, about 40 eminent European and American scholars founded the Mont Pélerin Society. Among them were Hayek, Mises, Raymond Aron, Michael Polanyi, Wilhelm Röpke, Milton Friedman, and Karl Popper. Those who identified with liberal ideas were no longer alone. The Foundation for Economic Education and the Mont Pélerin Society provided a reference and institutional framework for classical liberals and libertarians.

Mises's *Human Action* was another fundamental contribution to the revival of classical liberalism and to Rothbard's formation. In Mises's work, Rothbard found a wonderful economic framework that started from the simple axiom of individual human action, an action that is always a rational choice of means for the achievement of subjective ends. Mises's seminar in New York was an informal opportunity for those who believed in the free market to meet with one another. About half of the participants in Mises's seminar were libertarians who would constitute the first generation of Austrian economists in the United States and Austrian-derived libertarians.

Starting in the 1960s, the libertarian doctrine was consolidated, assuming autonomy and its own specific connotation. Rand made an important contribution to the definition of this philosophy, to the extent that in 1971 Jerome Tuccille published a volume with the eloquent title *It Usually Begins with Ayn Rand* (Tuccille, 1971). She was both a novelist and a philosopher, but her novels are characterized by strong philosophical and political content. Her first novel, *We the Living*, set in the Soviet Union, is the dramatic story of an unhappy love against the background of a strong opposition to communism (Rand, 1959). Kira Argounova, the protagonist, is the fervent anti-communist heroine; Leo Kovalensky represents the decadent Russian aristocrat, in love with Kira; and Andrei Taganov is the young idealist communist. At the end of the novel, Taganov's suicide represents the death of Marxist egalitarianism as a moral ideal. As Justin Raimondo notes, Rand had the exceptional ability to expound her philosophical and political ideas in a fictionalized form, without any trace of pedantry or didactics. *Anthem* is a dystopian novel that describes a collectivist society of the future, in which the individual is erased until he has only an acronym for a name and the word *I* is forbidden. Rand's dystopia is a collectivist and technologically backward society precisely because it has abolished individualism. Rand believed it is impossible that society can be at once politically repressive, collectivist, and at the same time technologically and economically developed, simply because individual creativity will have been nullified. To erase the individual is to give up creativity. The protagonist of the story rediscovers the forbidden word *I* and the electric light at the same time. The image of the light bulb emanating light is a symbol of the rediscovering of the self, linking progress and individualism.

Perhaps one of Rand's greatest and best-known masterpieces is *The Fountainhead*. The innovative architect Howard Roark represents the individualist and brilliant hero who must fight against the uniformed and conformist masses, which draw a "formidable circle" around the individual genius, much like in Tocqueville's description of mass society in *Democracy in America*. The monologue in which Howard Roark defends himself is famous and considered a manifesto of libertarian individualism.

Finally, *Atlas Shrugged* (Rand, 1989) describes an increasingly massified society, in which mechanical engineer John Galt and other industrialists, entrepreneurs, and scientists decide to protest limitations on individual initiative—a policy that can only lead to the destruction of wealth. Their protest consists of a strike, during which they gather in Gult's Gulch, an oasis in the Rocky Mountains, where they can freely express their creativity and initiative. In the background of the narrative is the "continuous confrontation between capitalist America and collectivist Russia, between the land of freedom, wealth, life and humanity on one side, land of slavery, misery, death and inhumanity on the other" (Thermes, 2021, p. 63). Eventually, following the mind strike, the American system descends into chaos. Seeing New York reduced to a dystopian ruin—similar to the aftermath of an atomic disaster—the Atlases decide to return to the outside world and rebuild America.

Alongside her work as a novelist, Rand was an essayist and philosopher. Among her most significant essays are *The Virtue of Selfishness* (Rand, 1964a), *Capitalism: The Unknown Ideal* (Rand, 1964b), *The New Left: The Anti-Industrial Revolution* (Rand, 1971), and *Introduction to Objectivist Epistemology* (Rand, 1979). Her other philosophical essays are contained in magazines she founded, such as *The Objectivist Newsletter*

(1962–1965), *The Objectivist* (1966–1971), and *The Ayn Rand Newsletter* (1971–1976). Randian objectivism is based on the observation of the nature of things according to a matrix of Aristotelian inspiration. It is from the observation of human nature that Rand arrives at a rationalist ethic based on selfishness—an egoism understood, however, in a particularly rich sense. Rand is a staunch supporter of the possibility of founding rational ethics on a solid epistemological basis and has, therefore, always been an enemy of ethical relativism. The ultimate goal of man as man—his end in itself—is life: "The standard of value of the Objectivist ethics—the standard by which one judges what is good or evil is *man's life*, or: that which is required for man's survival *qua* man. Since reason is man's basic means of survival, that which is proper to the life of a rational being is the good; that which negates, opposes or destroys it is the evil" (Rand, 1964, p. 25 *a*)—hence the rational Randian value system. These values are an expression of the individual's ability to sustain himself and progress through his own resources in a context of strong individual responsibility. Every human being is an end in itself and not a means to the ends of others; therefore, man must live for his own sake. "The Objectivist ethics holds that *human* good does not require human sacrifices and cannot be achieved by the sacrifice of anyone to anyone" (Rand, 1964, p. 34 *a*). Each individual must keep himself alive by his own efforts and act for his own self-interest. Objectivist ethics "proudly advocates and upholds *rational selfishness*—which means: the values required for man's survival *qua* man—which means: the values *required* for human survival" (Rand, 1964, p. 34 *a*). Selfishness must be understood in the sense that each individual has the right to cultivate himself without external interference. The ethics of altruism has given a strongly negative connotation to selfishness. For Rand, living for others by giving up one's own interest is not a value. Even when we engage in altruistic actions, we do so because of the value that certain people have for us—so the virtue of selfishness is expressed even in this case.

Objectivism exerted a strong appeal, especially among young right-wing students on American university campuses who did not identify with the New Right, often because its values were too conservative. Obviously, Rand's political theory derives from her objectivist ethics. Rand, politically, ranks among those libertarians defined as minarchists—supporters of a minimal state—whose only task is to defend against aggression and the administration of justice. Rand polemicized with Rothbard's anarchocapitalism, arguing that the sole purpose of a state is the protection of life, liberty, property, and the pursuit of happiness. The philosopher died in New York in 1982, but her thought was preserved first by Nathaniel and Barbara Branden and later by Leonard Peikoff.

Starting from the conceptual elaborations of Rand and Rothbard, libertarianism (see Tuccille, 1970; Hospers, 1971; Machan, 1975, 1989, 1994; Nash, 1976; Lemieux, 1983; Barry, 1986; Rasmussen & Uyl 1991; Machan & Rasmussen, 1995; Iannello, 1996; Colombatto, 1997; Di Robilant et al., 1998; Mingardi, 1999; Lottieri, 2001) has taken on its own very precise doctrinal connotation and has spread far beyond the borders of the United States, especially to Europe, both Western and Eastern, but also to Latin America. The circulation of ideas favored by the publication of now classic texts has certainly contributed to the diffusion of this line of thought, but so has the work of tireless think tanks such as the Ludwig von Mises Institute, the Cato Institute, and, among the youngest, the Istituto Bruno Leoni in Italy, just to name a few.

While libertarianism is united by such principles as support for the free market, methodological individualism, and distrust of the state, there are different positions among libertarians about the nature of a free society and the role of the state. There is a well-known difference between theorists of a minimal state—minarchists—such as Rand and Robert Nozick, on the one hand, and anarchocapitalists, who consider the state an immoral institution whose existence has no legitimate justification, on the other. What anarchocapitalists question is the very premise of modernity: the relationship between individual rights and the state. The ambiguity of modernity is in seeing the state as the solution to the problem of the best political regime, rather than a specific and possibly transient historical form of order. Libertarians include both minarchists and anarchocapitalists, such as Rothbard, Walter Block, Joseph Salerno, David Gordon, and Hans-Hermann Hoppe. Given this, it must be kept in mind that among libertarians there are profound differences not only regarding the legitimacy of the state but also from a gnoseological point of view—that is, the theoretical foundation of the rights of individuals and, consequently, of a free society. How is it possible to ethically justify the libertarian proposals for particular social and political forms of organization? It is possible to distinguish, on the one hand, a current that refers to the existence of ethical values and objective, rational, and universal individual rights and, on the other, a consequentialist approach. In the first case, the free society is defended as the only one compatible with rationally founded values and rights. To this strand belong all those authors who refer to rationalist theories of ethics—including, as we have seen, Rand and Rothbard, who supported a natural law libertarianism, Douglas Den Uyl and Douglas Rasmussen (Rasmussen & Uyl, 1991) who also refer to the tradition of natural law, and in general all the followers of Rothbard. Robert Nozick, for his part, defends his idea of the state as a simple night watchman, starting from a Kantian approach to rights.

In the consequentialist vein, however, the free society is defended on the basis that it can offer greater well-being, better satisfy individual preferences, and provide more efficient institutions. This strand includes those who defend freedom on the basis of economic and utilitarian considerations in the wake of Mises, such as David Friedman, Leland B. Yeager, and Charles Murray.

At the heart of the American conservatism of the New Right was the war on communism, and anyone who did not agree with the policies involving that war was expelled from the conservative movement. But that wasn't all: as Raimondo notes, it seemed that the idea of noninterventionism in foreign policy had emerged among the conservative right for the first time. In this way, the entire tradition of the Old Right was forgotten (Raimondo, 2014, p. 224). It is well known that during the presidency of John F. Kennedy, the United States went so far as to risk a war with the Soviet Union over the Cuban question and found itself embroiled for years in the war in Vietnam. In this crusade against communism, the New Right was committed to increasing the power of the state and the executive.

What profoundly marked Rothbardian thought and militancy was the commitment of the United States in the Vietnam War. It is worth dwelling on what happened between 1963 and 1975, since these were years that brought to maturity Rothbard's detachment from the New Right and the formation of a conscious libertarian movement that was independent and decidedly opposed to any military and imperialist commitment of the United States in foreign policy. With the Cold War, the United States administration saw the Ho Chi Minh government and Vietnam as tools for the expansion of the Soviet Union's power in East Asia. The United States helped Vietnam, temporarily divided between North and South, establish a noncommunist government in South Vietnam, which was supposed to function as a bulwark against further communist expansion in the region. But when North Vietnam seemed to have the upper hand over the South, Kennedy authorized the overthrow of the Southern government in 1963. Faced with the possible collapse of South Vietnam, Kennedy's successor,

Lyndon Johnson, began bombing North Vietnam and drafting American soldiers in 1965. Between 1965 and 1972, the war saw the escalation of US involvement and became the main international conflict. Such involvement proved counterproductive to the attempt to build a stable, pro-American government in South Vietnam. In addition, the army of the South did not receive any preparation to withstand the attacks of the North. At this point, in the United States, peace movements had begun to mobilize, and a general discontent was spreading among the population over the ever-increasing costs of war, in terms of both money and human lives. In Washington and major American cities, there were protests against the war. In October 1967, about fifty thousand citizens marched to the Pentagon to express their discontent and opposition to the war, which was perceived as something far away and unnecessarily calling young Americans to die in the swamps of Vietnam. President Johnson imposed new taxes to support the war effort, and many members of Congress, both Democrats and Republicans, abandoned him, leaving him increasingly isolated. After the failure of attempts to negotiate peace in 1968 in Paris, Johnson's successor, Republican Richard Nixon, facing increasingly pressing demands from American citizens, began a new policy that provided for the gradual exit from Vietnam. He sought to increase aid to the South Vietnamese army in terms of training and autonomy in fighting. At the same time, however, he ordered the bombing of North Vietnamese bases in Cambodia. During the Nixon presidency, American anti-war protest grew into a gigantic demonstration in Washington in the spring of 1971 calling for an end to the war. Peace talks began in 1972, and the treaty for the withdrawal of American troops from Vietnam was signed in January 1973. Subsequently, President Nixon, engulfed in the Watergate scandal, resigned in 1974. Secretary of State Henry Kissinger carried out the gradual return of the Americans to their homeland. All this resulted in the decisive demoralization of South Vietnam, whose army had been destroyed. There was nothing left to do but evacuate the remaining American personnel and those Vietnamese who continued to support the United States. As Saigon collapsed under attacks from the North, the evacuation was carried out in a panic by helicopters fleeing from the roof of the American embassy, a sequence of events that recurred recently with the withdrawal of Americans from Afghanistan.

The cost of this long war for the United States was very high. The Vietnam Veterans Memorial in Washington records the names of more than fifty-eight thousand Americans who died or went missing.

The wounded were about three hundred thousand, while the economic costs are around $167 billion. The Vietnam War, along with the Watergate scandal, only increased distrust of government, institutions, and power. All this can be found not only in Rothbardian militancy—in his momentary alliance with the youth protest movement of the New Left—but also in his writings, including his 1965 article "Left and Right: The Prospect for Liberty," one of the foundations of the magazine *Left and Right: A Journal of Libertarian Thought*, and, above all, *For a New Liberty: The Libertarian Manifesto* (Rothbard, 1973). In 1972, the time was ripe for the birth of the Libertarian Party, and libertarians redefined themselves autonomously from both the American Right and the Left at a critical moment in American history. Randians and libertarians grew and flourished as movements outside conservatism and the New Right. At the instigation of Charles Koch, to Rothbard's delight, the Cato Institute was born.

The history of the conservative movement after Nixon's capitulation culminated with the rise of Ronald Reagan within the Republican Party, which also heralded his winning the presidency in 1980. From the point of view of economic policy, the Reagan presidency was characterized by a classical liberal orientation—including deregulation, liberalization, and the reduction of the tax burden—as well as the reduction of bureaucracy and its role in the lives of citizens. Reagan's foreign policy focused on developing a technological and military challenge to the Soviet Union, which was defined as the evil empire. Symbolic of this policy was the Strategic Defense Initiative, although it was never developed and deployed. In the second half of the 1980s, Reagan began talks and negotiations with President Mikhail Gorbachev that aimed to reduce atomic weapons and inaugurate a new era of world peace. The collapse of the Berlin Wall made 1989 a symbolic year. A few months after the event—and after the inauguration of Reagan's successor to the presidency, George H. W. Bush—the Soviet Union, and with it the states that were in its orbit, began to collapse.

With the end of the Cold War, the communist enemy was no longer a significant force, and it was time to begin a movement that would recover with renewed vigor the values of the Old Right—that would clearly oppose the idea that the United States should be the guardian of the world and leader in international aid. For Rothbard, it was time to recreate the Old Right movement, which in the 1990s identified with paleolibertarianism. On the other side of the conservative political spectrum, the neoconservatives for their part maintained the principle of interventionism in foreign policy and the ideal of the welfare state, continuing to support big government to promote a kind of global democracy (Kaplan & Kristol, 2003; Podhoretz, 2007).

Among the most prominent protagonists of the paleoconservative movement were Patrick J. Buchanan and Paul Gottfried. The identification with the *paleo* prefix by an important group of conservatives and libertarians, including Rothbard himself, meant nothing more than wanting to recover the legacy of the Old Right—Nock, Mencken, Chodorov, Wilder Lane, and so on, as well as noninterventionism and anti-imperialism in foreign policy. The position of paleoconservatives emerged in all its force during the first Gulf War—a military intervention of the United States against Saddam Hussein's Iraq, which in August 1990 had invaded Kuwait, proclaiming it a province of Iraq—which they strongly opposed, clashing with the Bush presidency. Rothbard consistently spoke out against intervention in Iraq (Rockwell, 2000). The neoconservatives, for their part, supported the famous Operation Desert Storm, led by General Norman Schwarzkopf in command of a United Nations coalition. On February 28, 1991, the war operations ended victoriously, and American soldiers were hailed at home as heroes. But the paleoconservatives and paleolibertarians were against big government, increasing taxation, foreign aid, and the export of democracy. They continued to advocate free markets, lower taxes, and noninterventionism in foreign policy.

References

Barry, N. P. (1986). *On classical liberalism and libertarianism.* Macmillan.

Bassani, L. M. (1996). L'anarcocapitalismo di Murray Newton Rothbard, in M. N. Rothbard, *L'etica della Libertà.* Liberilibri.

Bassani, L. M. (2004). *Introduzione* in *Per una nuova libertà: il manifesto libertario*, Liberilibri.

Block, W., & Rockwell, L. H. (Eds.). (1988). *Man, economy, and liberty: Essays in honor of Murray N. Rothbard.* Ludwig von Mises Institute.

Casey, G. (2010). *Murray Rothbard.* Bloomsbury.

Colombatto, E. (1997). *Economia di mercato, stato di diritto e intervento pubblico. Biblioteca della libertà*, 140.

Di Robilant, E., Cavalla, F., Ricossa, S., & Angeletti, A. (1998). *Contro lo Stato massimo.* Liberilibri.

Friedman, M. (1946). *Roofs or Ceilings?* Foundation for Economic Education.

Gordon, D. (2007). *The Essential Rothbard.* Ludwig von Mises Institute.

Hayek, F. A. V. (1944). *The Road to Serfdom*. George Routledge & Sons.
Hoppe, H. H. (1998). *Introduction* to *The ethics of liberty*, M. N. Rothbard, New York University Press.
Hospers, J. (1971). *Libertarianism: A political philosophy for tomorrow*. Nash Publishing.
Iannello, N. (1996). Liberisti, liberali, liberal, libertari … . *Biblioteca della libertà*, 133.
Iannello, N. (2017). La scienza politica di un economista: Scambio e potere secondo Murray N. Rothbard. In M. N. Rothbard, *Potere e mercato: lo Stato e L'economia*. IBL Libri.
Kaplan, L., & Kristol, W. (2003). *The war over Iraq: Saddams's Tyranny and America's mission*. Encounter.
Lemieux, P. (1983). *Liberalisme À L'anarchocapitalisme*. Presses Universitaires de France.
Lottieri, C. (2001). *Il Pensiero libertario contemporaneo*. Liberilibri.
Machan, T. R. (1975). *Human rights and human liberties*. Nelson-Hall.
Machan, T. R. (1989). *Individuals and their rights*. Open Court.
Machan, T. R. (1994). *Private rights, public illusions*. Transaction.
Machan, T. R., & Rasmussen, D. (Eds.). (1995). *Liberty for the twenty-first century: Contemporary libertarian thought*. Rowan & Littlefield.
Marcognat, F. (2012). *Murray Rothbard*. Edilivre.
Mingardi, A. (1999). *Estremisti della libertà*. L. Facco.
Mises, L. V. (1944a). *Bureaucracy*. Yale University Press.
Mises, L. V. (1944b). *Omnipotent Government*. Yale University Press.
Mises, L. V. (1998). *Human Action: A Treatise on Economics*. Ludwig von Mises Institute, Original work published 1949.
Modugno, R. A. (2009). (Ed.). *Rothbard Vs. the philosophers: Unpublished writings on Hayek, Mises, Strauss, and Polanyi*. Ludwig von Mises Institute.
Modugno, R. A. (1998). *Murray N. Rothbard e l'anarco-capitalismo americano*. Rubbettino.
Modugno, R. A. (2019). The libertarian legacy of the old right: Democracy and representative government. *Journal of Libertarian Studies*, *23*, 5–21.
Modugno, R. A. (Ed.). (Forthcoming). *Murray Rothbard on politics, philosophy, and history: A selection from his papers*. Ludwig von Mises Institute *(a)*.
Modugno, R. A. (Forthcoming). The Rothbard papers: The genesis of Murray N. Rothbard's Philosophical, political and theoretical thought. In R. A. Modugno. (Ed.). *Murray Rothbard on Politics, Philosophy, and History: A Selection from His Papers*. Ludwig von Mises Institute *(b)*.
Nash, G. H. (1976). *The conservative intellectual movement in America since 1945*. Basic Books.
Podhoretz, N. (2007). *World War IV: The long struggle against islamofascism*. Doubleday.

Raimondo, J. (2000). *An enemy of the state: The life of Murray N. Rothbard.* Prometheus.

Raimondo, J. (2014). *Reclaiming the American right: The lost legacy of the conservative movement.* ISI Books.

Rand, A. (1938). *Anthem.* Cassel.

Rand, A. (1959). *We the living.* Random House.

Rand, A. (1964a). *The virtue of selfishness.* Signet.

Rand, A. (1964b). *Capitalism: The unknown ideal.* New American Library.

Rand, A. (1971). *The New Left: The Anti-Industrial Revolution.* New American Library.

Rand, A. (1979). *Introduction to objectivist epistemology.* New American Library.

Rand, A. (1989). *Atlas shrugged.* Easton Press, Original work published 1957.

Rand, A. (1994). *The fountainhead.* Plume, Original work published 1943.

Rasmussen, D., & den Uyl, D. (1991). *Liberty and nature: An aristotelian defense of liberal order.* Open Court.

Rockwell, L. H. (Ed.). (1995). Murray N. In *Rothbard: In Memoriam.* Ludwig von Mises Institute.

Rockwell, L. H. (Ed.). (2000). *The irrepressible Rothbard: The Rothbard-Rockwell report: essays of Murray N. Rothbard.* Center for Libertarian Studies.

Rothbard, M. N. (1962). *The panic of 1819.* Columbia University Press.

Rothbard, M. N. (1973). *For a new liberty: The libertarian manifesto.* Macmillan.

Rothbard, M. N. (1988). What's wrong with the liberty poll, or, how i became a libertarian. *Liberty, 53.*

Rothbard, M. N. (1994). Nations by consent: Decomposing the nation-state. *Journal of Libertarian Studies, 11*(1), 1–10.

Rothbard, M. N. (2000). A strategy for the right. In L. H. Rockwell (Ed.), *The irrepressible rothbard: The rothbard-rockwell report.* Essays of Murray N. Rothbard. Center for Libertarian Studies.

Rothbard, M. N. (2007). *The betrayal of the American right.* Ludwig Von Mises Institute.

Thermes, D. (2021). *Ayn Rand e il fascismo eterno: una narrazione distopica.* IBL Libri.

Tuccille, J. (1970). *Radical libertarianism: A right wing alternative.* Bobbs-Merrill.

Tuccille, J. (1971). *It usually begins with ayn rand.* Fox and Wilkes.

Vaughn, K. (1994). *Austrian economics in America: The migration of a tradition.* Cambridge University Press.

von, Kuehnelt-Leddihn, E. (1953). Resurgence of liberalism *freeman*, pp. 337–339.

CHAPTER 3

Rothbard, the Economist

Keywords Apriorism · Praxeology · Natural law · Catholicism · Austrian cycle · Great depression · New deal · Anarchocapitalism · Democracy

1 Methodological Premises and Economic Analyses

Now that we have outlined the context and personal experiences of Rothbard, we have the necessary basis for examining his work and thought. First, it should be emphasized that Rothbard, although deeply influenced by Mises and the Austrian school, combined these influences with the Old Right culture to which he was deeply attached and with the natural law tradition that permeated the American classical liberal culture of the founding fathers and Thomas Jefferson. From all this, as we will see, emerges a reworking and, in part, a revision of the Austrian school that is particularly original.

One of the first papers to consider is Rothbard's "In Defense of 'Extreme Apriorism'," which appeared in 1957 in the *Southern Economics Journal.* It defends and supports "praxeology," Mises's theory of human action. Praxeology contains a fundamental axiom: the existence of human action. Economics is the study of human action, which is always economic insofar as it involves rational choices of means to accomplish ends that, for Mises, are always subjective. The axiom of human action,

R. A. Modugno, *The Legacy of Murray N. Rothbard*, Palgrave Studies in Austrian Economics,
https://doi.org/10.1007/978-3-032-06870-5_3

Rothbard explains, is a priori, a self-evident reality. From this axiom derive some postulates, such as the scarcity of resources, the division of labor, the time factor as a resource, the means–ends relationship, and the law of diminishing marginal utility. From these, Mises deduces the whole of economic science. Rothbard specifies that Mises assumes only that man acts on the basis of his ends and uses means to realize them. At this point, however, Rothbard, while fully sharing the a priori Misesian approach, introduces a clarification that will be the basis of his detachment from Mises's avalutative approach to human ends and begins a typically Rothbardian tradition.

> Whether we consider the Action Axiom "a priori" or "empirical" depends on our ultimate philosophical position. Professor Mises, in the neo-Kantian tradition, considers this axiom a *law of thought* and therefore a categorical truth a priori to all experience. My own epistemological position rests on Aristotle and St. Thomas rather than Kant, and hence I would interpret the proposition differently. I would consider the axiom a *law of reality* rather than a law of thought, and hence "empirical" rather than "a priori." But it should be obvious that this type of "empiricism" is so out of step with modern empiricism that I may just as well continue to call it *a priori* for present purposes. (Rothbard, 1957, pp. 317–318 *b*. See Gordon, 1993, 2004)

In reality, this path of rediscovery and revaluation of the concept of human nature—on which he would base his ethics of freedom—had already been undertaken by Rothbard in a paper written in 1954, called "The Concepts 'Rational' and 'Irrational'," in which the search for the possibility of a rational foundation of ethics is clear. The criticism of Mises's avalutative approach to human action is already evident, understood as a rational choice of means that are always subjective. The concepts of rational and irrational should, in Rothbard's view, apply to both means and ends. "I believe, furthermore, that the concepts of 'rational' and 'irrational' are not only applicable to means but also to *ends*. This is the domain of the discipline of the philosophy of *ethics* … . Certain general rules for the achievement of happiness can be laid down on a scientific basis, i.e., our scientific knowledge of the nature of man. On the basis of what is best for man, we can elaborate general criteria of ends" (Rothbard, 1954, forthcoming). As Justin Raimondo notes, Rothbard did not begin associating with Ayn Rand until 1954 (Raimondo, 2000, p. 109). It is not necessarily obvious, therefore, that the idea of the recovery of the concept of human nature and the natural law of the Aristotelian-Thomist matrix was influenced by Rand's knowledge, since the paper is from March 1954. Rothbard never recognized this possibility, and the matter remains unclear.

Two other very important Rothbard works appeared, like others, after his death. These are the two substantial volumes *Economic Thought before Adam Smith and Classical Economics*, both published in 1995, in which he presents a detailed and scholarly account of the history of economic thought from an Austrian perspective. In this work, the real heroes are the late Spanish Scholastics of the School of Salamanca of the sixteenth century, who had developed a subjective theory of value, as did later scholars such as Cantillon, Turgot, and Say.

The Rothbardian studies on the late Spanish Scholastics of the School of Salamanca actually date back to 1957, much earlier than 1995 and even 1976. One of the most successful explanations within the history of the social sciences is Max Weber's explanation of the nature and spirit of capitalism. In his *The Protestant Ethic and the Spirit of Capitalism*, trade, labor, and free and autonomous enterprise become part of a new social order. Historically, the tenacious and prolonged use of intelligence, imagination, and industriousness is the great novelty brought by the spirit of capitalism. Weber directly links the prominence of such moral virtues to Protestant, Calvinist, Puritan ethics (Weber, 2002). In a 1957 memorandum on Catholicism, Protestantism, and capitalism (Chapter 4), Rothbard writes: "The standard interpretation runs about as follows: ... the Calvinist spirit and ethic, emphasizing the positive value of hard work, thrift, and money-making, led to a flowering of capitalism as compared to Catholic frowning on money-making; laissez-faire economics grew in the Protestant atmosphere of Britain (Adam Smith, etc.)" (Rothbard, 1957a, forthcoming).

Max Weber had the merit of having sensed the moral dimension of economic action and consequently of having emphasized some forms of the human spirit indispensable for the correct understanding of entrepreneurial activity, such as organization, industriousness, discipline, and the spirit of initiative. But in reality, regarding the conception of the human mind, inventiveness, knowledge, skills, the spirit of initiative, and the predisposition to cooperation and collaboration, we owe a great intellectual debt to the notion developed by the medieval canonist fathers, and in particular by the Franciscan friar Peter John Olivi (1248–1298)

(Tierney, 1997). Moreover, the documentation made known by some British, American, and Italian historians leads us to believe that the cultural foundations of modern capitalism go back to a historical period that precedes the Protestant Reformation by several centuries. They are in fact found in the phenomenon of medieval Italian towns of the fourteenth century, in the birth of early medieval civil society, and in the life conducted within the Benedictine monasteries, roots that were then taken up and amplified by the late Spanish scholastics of the School of Salamanca of the sixteenth and seventeenth centuries (Bazzicchi, 2003; Block et al., 1985; de Roover, 1967; Nuccio, 1995).

In 1976, nineteen years after the memorandum of 1957, an innovative essay by Rothbard entitled "New Light on the Prehistory of the Austrian School" was published in which Rothbard showed that he fully accepted the thesis of the Catholic and scholastic origins of capitalism and the Austrian school of economics (Rothbard, 1976). This is the same clear position advocated in *An Austrian Perspective on the History of Economic Thought* of 1995. In the 1957 paper, Rothbard cites authors such as Marjorie Grice-Hutchinson (Grice-Hutchinson, 2009), Emil Kauder (Kauder, 1953a, pp. 638–650, 1953b pp. 564–575), and Raymond de Roover (De Roover, 1955, pp. 161–190), whom we will also find in the subsequent writings of 1976 and 1995. The 1957 memorandum proves to be fundamental to understanding the Rothbardian transition from the mainstream conception of the Weberian link between Protestantism and the spirit of capitalism to a completely different conception of the roots of capitalism and the Austrian school that considers the medieval Italian cities, the medieval canonists, and the late scholastics of the School of Salamanca as the authentic protagonists. Rothbard wrote in the 1957 memorandum:

"We may sum up the Case for Catholicism as follows:

1. Smith's laissez-faire and natural law views descended from the late Scholastics, and from the Catholic Physiocrats
2. The Catholics had developed marginal utility, subjective value economics, and the idea that the just price was the market price, while the British Protestants grafted on a dangerous and ultimately highly statist labor theory of value, influenced by Calvinism
3. Some of the most "dogmatic" laissez-faire theorists have been Catholics: from the Physiocrats to Bastiat

4. Capitalism began in the Catholic Italian cities of the fourteenth century
5. Natural rights and other rationalist views descended from the Scholastics."

We are faced with the exact moment of the transition from one conception to another. In fact, Rothbard himself declares that he is not yet ready to abandon Weber's thesis altogether but finds the new discoveries particularly convincing, stating that "it seems evident that the story is far more complex than the standard view believes" (Rothbard, 1957a, forthcoming).

Rothbard searched, therefore, for the roots of the Austrian school of economics in the works of Spanish scholastics from the mid-sixteenth to the seventeenth century. Most of the scholastics who taught morals and theology at the University of Salamanca, mainly Dominicans and Jesuits, were able to elaborate on the subjectivist and liberal tradition which, two and a half centuries later, Carl Menger and his followers would consider as the basis of the Austrian school. Among them, we have the founder of the School of Salamanca, Francisco de Vitoria (1485–1546), the Dominican Domingo de Soto (1494–1560), the Jesuit Luis de Molina (1535–1600), and Diego de Covarrubias (1512–1577).

2 Rothbard, the Mises Scholar

In the wake of reading *Human Action* and assiduous attendance of Mises's seminar, Rothbard published one of the most comprehensible and comprehensive expositions of Austrian school economics: *Man, Economy, and State* (Rothbard, 1962). The volume clarifies the fundamental elements of human action from which the whole economic theory is deduced. Praxeology is the scientific study of human action, which is a kind of action aimed at the realization of an end. The human being acts whenever he uses means to achieve an end that is always subjective. The propositions that are deduced from the undeniable axiom that human beings exist and act are true a priori—that is, they do not need any proof. All actions involve an exchange or a choice, since the doer seeks to reach a better state of affairs than he would have achieved if he had acted differently. Only individuals act, because only individuals can evaluate different options and make choices. Every action takes place at a specific time, and every action is future-oriented, in the sense that every action seeks to create better future conditions—always from their subjective point of view—for those who act. Implicit in every action is uncertainty about the future, and entrepreneurial activity in particular implies dealing with this uncertainty and trying to predict what the future conditions will be. Already from the beginning of the first volume, Rothbard considers the *Robinson Crusoe* scenario unrealistic, despite its popularity in previous treatises on economics by other authors. Austrian economics insists on studying the behavior of the individual only to discover a priori truths that are useful for the study of human behavior within society.

Voluntary exchange implies that the parties involved are convinced that they are benefiting from the exchange. Here, Rothbard clearly follows Mises, emphasizing that the sense of community and altruism are the result, and not the cause, of social cooperation and the maximum productivity made possible by the division of labor, which is nothing more than a form of cooperation between individuals. At this point, Rothbard introduces catallaxis, which is that branch of praxeology dealing with monetary exchange. The price or purchasing power of money is that set of goods and services for which a unit of money can be exchanged. Mises was the first economist to apply the theory of subjective marginal utility to money, something that economists had previously applied only to barter.

Another concept introduced by Mises and taken up by Rothbard is the uniformly rotating economy—that is, a situation in which all discomfort has been removed in order to study interpersonal exchange and the difference between profit and interest. In such a model of the structure of production, capitalists advance their money to the owners of the factors of production so they can sell goods to consumers in the future. Capitalists earn more from consumers than they have paid to the owners of all factors of production. But for an economist, this is not a profit but an interest earned from investment. The first lesson to be drawn from this is that all income from selling to a consumer can be traced back to the owners of the factors of production. The real challenge is production. Once the necessary goods have been produced, it is easy to get people to buy them.

A fundamental point of *Man, Economy, and State* challenges the Keynesian paradox of savings: to accumulate capital and produce a greater volume of goods, it is necessary to reduce consumption at present. But if retailers see a decline in demand for their products, why should they invest in the future? Only Austrian economic theory, which incorporates time into production, can resolve this paradox. As Böhm-Bawerk himself replied, when people save, spending less in the present, they do so in the hope that they can spend more in the future. Another fundamental difference from Keynesian economics is that the Austrian school does not start from the assumption of full employment but from the consideration that individuals willing to work, even for a low wage, will always be able to find a job. Moreover, prices determine costs and not the other way around, and prices always emerge from the point of view of the individual. Consumer valuations determine the marginal utility of consumer goods and ultimately their prices. In *Man, Economy, and State*, Rothbard criticizes Mises for using the concept of consumer sovereignty as an overly political metaphor. For Rothbard, in a free market, individuals have full control over their bodies and property.

The last part *of Man, Economy, and State* is dedicated to violent intervention in the market by the state. Rothbard analyzes the effects of violating private property rights and, in particular, violations committed by the state—that is, interventionism, intrusion, and violence in civil society. Rothbard introduces his own original definitions of the types of such violations. Autistic intervention is the use of force against a single individual and does not involve others; binary intervention occurs when the aggressor establishes a hegemonic relationship over the victim; and triangular intervention occurs when the aggressor uses force to alter the relationship between two subjects. State intervention in the market always harms at least one individual, and the end result will always be to distort the economy. Price controls, for example, alter the exchange of goods and services between individuals. A cap on prices leads to scarcity of the goods and services whose prices are controlled. A minimum price also leads to scarcity, as, for example, when the state creates unemployment by imposing a minimum wage. Both taxation and government spending distort the economy: taxation diverts resources that could have been used fruitfully from the private sector, while government spending, which is based on credit expansion and an artificial lowering of interest rates, discourages saving. There will be a momentary period of apparent well-being as citizens increase their consumption; but without a genuine increase in savings, the capital structure will at some point become unbalanced, and entrepreneurs will be unable to realize their plans. The theme of violent state intervention in the economy should have been the last part of *Man, Economy, and State*, but the publisher objected that the volume, already quite substantial, would be too long. Rothbard reduced the theme to a summary found in Chapter 12, but he devoted a separate work to it in

Power and Market, published in 1970, completing the analysis begun in *Man, Economy, and State.*

3 The Great Depression of 1929 as the Failure of Capitalism? Another Explanation is Possible

Rothbard's *America's Great Depression* (Rothbard, 1963) is fundamental to understanding the real causes of the Great Depression, which, beginning in 1929, shook the United States and the entire Western world, leaving an indelible trauma in American history and impressing on the psychology of all humanity a distrust toward capitalism and the free market. Through the economics of the Austrian school, Rothbard deconstructs the myth that the Great Depression constitutes irrefutable evidence of the failure of free market capitalism. He instead illustrates the dangers of government interference in the economy. The economic collapse of 1929 was nothing more than a necessary correction and a direct consequence of the completely artificial boom of the Roaring Twenties induced by the Federal Reserve's policy of monetary expansion. The government's subsequent attempts to remedy the disaster only worsened the situation. Rothbard was a pioneer of revisionism concerning President Herbert Hoover—in fact, contrary to the myth that Hoover was an opponent of big government, Rothbard claims that it was precisely his political and economic engineering that paved the way for Roosevelt's New Deal.

Rothbard's work applies Ludwig von Mises's business cycle theory to the long incubation and the advent of the Great Depression. He expounds the theory and considers the history of the policy implemented by the Federal Reserve during the 1920s, highlighting the crucial role of Benjamin Strong (1872–1928), governor of the Federal Reserve Bank of New York, and his policy of monetary expansion, which was partly motivated by a desire to help Britain support the pound. Strong was a close friend of Montagu Norman (1871–1950), governor of the Bank of England. After the collapse of 1929, Hoover followed an interventionist policy that foreshadowed the New Deal. Against the popular stereotype, Rothbard shows that the president was by no means a supporter of laissez-faire—for example, he kept wages artificially high, thus contributing to the exponential growth of unemployment.

Economic fluctuations within certain sectors are normal. Skilled entrepreneurs can predict such changes in social and economic conditions.

Mises's theory of the business cycle, on the other hand, tries to understand a different phenomenon—namely the expansion, boom, and subsequent depression of an entire economy. "The main problem that a theory of depression must explain is: *why is there a sudden general cluster of business errors*? This is the first question for any cycle theory … . How, then, do we explain the curious phenomenon of the crisis when almost all entrepreneurs suffer sudden losses? In short, how did all the country's astute businessmen come to make such errors together, and why were they all suddenly revealed at this particular time? This is the great problem of cycle theory" (Rothbard, 1963, p. 8). According to Austrian economic theory, people, to varying degrees, prefer to have some goods sooner rather than later. This time preference rate determines the natural rate of interest. The interest rates on loans set by banks reflect these natural rates. But manipulating the quantity of money in the market—for example, an expansion of bank credit to businesses—lowers the interest rate below the natural rate. As a result, entrepreneurs, seeing the availability of money at low interest rates, will be encouraged to invest in longer production processes, resulting in an investment boom. But since such an interest rate does not reflect people's time preferences, the interest rate will rise and many of the new investments will prove unsustainable and fail. These failures represent the phenomenon of depression—that is, the depression phase of the economic cycle. In Mises's view, such a depression—the failure of bad investments—is in fact beneficial because it allows the market to make the necessary adjustments to meet consumers' time preferences. The government, therefore, should not interfere with this phase. Government interventions, further monetary expansions, subsidies, minimum wages, and bailouts of failing businesses will only turn one phase of the business cycle into an increasingly long and painful depression.

Rothbard saw in Roosevelt's New Deal the logical extension of Hoover's policies and the First World War—namely a government increasingly invasive in the economy and society. The New Deal—with its imposition of a corporatist state, dominated by big business and powerful labor organizations, and allied with intellectuals ready to forge the rhetoric of the welfare state—was perceived by individualist libertarians as the entry of fascism into the United States. At this point, they watched with dismay and bitterness as the progressives embraced the apology of the New Deal to the point of deification (Rothbard, 2007, pp. 23–24).

"As 1931 drew to a close and another Congressional session drew near, the country and indeed the world were in the midst of an authentic crisis atmosphere—a crisis of policy and of ideology. The depression, so long in effect, was now rapidly growing worse, in America and throughout the world. The stage was set for" what Rothbard called "the 'Hoover New Deal' of 1932" (Rothbard, 1963, p. 284). In the Rothbardian reconstruction of those crucial years, there was in fact a New Deal that anticipated Roosevelt's and can be attributed to Hoover. Few understood that the National Recovery Administration, established in 1933 by Roosevelt, and the Agricultural Adjustment Act were nothing more than the results of collectivist programs favored by big business, such as the famous Swope plan, conceived by Gerard Swope in 1931 and adopted by major American industries the following year. The business world was thinking about collectivist plans as a way to end the depression. In September 1931, Gerald Swope, president of General Electric, presented the Swope plan at a National Recovery Administration meeting. Each productive sector was to be forcibly organized into trade associations under federal control to regulate and stabilize prices and production and to impose appropriate commercial practices. In general, the federal government, with the help of a joint body of managers and employees representing the national economy, would coordinate production and consumption. The Federal Trade Commission would oversee trade associations for all companies with at least 50 employees. Workers would receive life insurance, pensions, and unemployment insurance, paid in part by employers. The American Chamber of Commerce backed the plan (Rothbard, 1963, pp. 277–282). The influential historian Charles A. Beard denounced laissez-faire and called for a five-year plan of industrial cartelization. One of the main proponents of the cartelization was Bernard M. Baruch, a Wall Street financier. Collectivist ideas seemed to have spread to different parts of the business and financial world since the beginning of the Great Depression in 1929. Hoover criticized the Swope plan for being inefficient, monopolistic, and mandatory, denying his support. "It was also to Hoover's credit—Rothbard writes—that he resisted the pressure of Henry Harriman, who urged Hoover to adopt the Swope Plan for economic fascism during his campaign, a plan which was soon to bear fruit in the National Recovery Administration (NRA)" (Rothbard, 1963, p. 323). Roosevelt declared himself in favor, but Hoover's own policy increasingly slipped toward interventionism and statism. The Chamber of Commerce demanded public works and federal subsidies. A joint committee of the National Association of Manufacturers and the National Industrial Council called for more public works and intervention in the purchasing power of the dollar. In October, the American Federation of Labor adopted a radical Emergency Unemployment Program and welcomed Hoover's policy of maintaining wages and reducing working hours. Meanwhile, states began to make the cartelization of the oil industry mandatory (Rothbard, 1963, p. 283).

Hoover urged more drastic action, and he presented the following program:

1. Establish a Reconstruction Finance Corporation, which would use treasury funds to lend to banks, industries, agricultural credit agencies, and local governments.
2. Broaden the eligibility requirement for discounting at the Fed.
3. Create a home loan bank discount system to revive construction and employment measures which had been warmly endorsed by a National Housing Conference recently convened by Hoover for that purpose.
4. Expand government aid to Federal Land Banks.
5. Set up a Public Works Administration to coordinate and expand Federal public works.
6. Legalize Hoover's order restricting immigration.
7. Do something to weaken "destructive competition" (i.e., competition) in natural resource use.
8. Grant direct loans of $300 million to states for relief.
9. Reform the bankruptcy laws (i.e., weaken protection for the creditor).

Hoover was also anxious to "protect railroads from unregulated competition" and to subsidize failing railroads. In addition, he called for labor-splitting programs to save millions of Americans from unemployment (Rothbard, 1963, pp. 285–286).

All this translated primarily to a sharp increase in taxation. Taxes on income and real estate were drastically increased, which decreased consumption. The property tax was doubled and the exemption threshold halved. The gift and inheritance tax, which had been eliminated, was gradually reintroduced. "Many wartime excise taxes were revived" (Rothbard, 1963, p. 286). Nevertheless, federal revenues declined during 1932 due to the worsening depression, which was itself largely caused by the increased tax burden. "Despite the drastic increase in tax rates, total Federal revenue for 1932 declined because of the deepened depression—itself partly caused by the increase in tax rates. Total Federal receipts, excluding government enterprises, declined from $2.2 billion in 1931 to $1.9 billion in 1932; including government enterprises, Federal receipts fell from $3.4 billion to $3 billion. Total government receipts fell from $12.4 billion to $11.5 billion including government enterprises, from $10.3 billion to $9.5 billion excluding them" (Rothbard, 1963, p. 288). At the same time, Congress and economists were pushing for more public works with increased government spending, which was considered the main way out of the depression. From the construction sector came suggestions for substantial public spending that would be concentrated mainly in public works, and in general there was pressure for economic central planning. Hoover himself, however, had to admit that his program to double federal construction had been a failure. His preference shifted at this point to federal subsidies for the states. But in reality he never put a stop to the abundant loans being granted to large public works, such as dams, toll bridges, and building renovations. The approval of the Emergency Relief and Construction Act of July 1932 was "the nation's first Federal relief legislation" (Rothbard, 1963, p. 300). Hoover insisted on launching a grand inflationary plan, creating more low-interest money. The president launched "a huge inflationist program," which turned into a resounding defeat: "The drop in gold demanded a reduction in the money supply to maintain public confidence in the dollar and in the banking system; the increase of money in circulation out of season was an ominous sign that the public was losing confidence in the banks … . The artificial cheap money policy in 1932 greatly lowered interest rates all-around, and therefore further discouraged the banks from making loans or investments" (Rothbard, 1963, pp. 301–303).

With the end of his term and during the election campaign, Hoover "staunchly upheld a protective tariff during his campaign, and declared that his administration had successfully kept American farm prices above world prices, aided by tariffs on agricultural products. He did not seem to see that this price-raising reduced foreign demand for American farm products. He hailed work-sharing without seeing that it perpetuated unemployment, and spoke proudly of the artificial expansion by business of construction 'beyond present needs' at his request in 1929–30, without seeing the resulting malinvestment and business losses" (Rothbard, 1963, p. 322). And again, Rothbard points out that:

> for the first time, laissez-faire was boldly thrown overboard and every governmental weapon thrown into the breach. America had awakened, and was now ready to use the State to the hilt, unhampered by the supposed shibboleths of laissez-faire. President Hoover was a bold and audacious leader in this awakening. By every "progressive" tenet of our day, he should have ended his term a conquering hero; instead he left America in utter and complete ruin—a ruin unprecedented in length and intensity. What was the trouble? Economic theory demonstrates that only governmental inflation can generate a boom-and-bust cycle, and that the depression will be prolonged and aggravated by inflationist and other interventionary measures. In contrast to the myth of laissez-faire, we have shown in this book how government intervention generated the unsound boom of the 1920s, and how Hoover's new departure aggravated the Great Depression by massive measures of interference. The guilt for the Great Depression must, at long last, be lifted from the shoulders of the free-market economy, and placed where it properly belongs: at the doors of politicians, bureaucrats, and the mass of "enlightened" economists. And in any other depression, past or future, the story will be the same. (Rothbard, 1963, pp. 336-337)

These quotes express a great lesson based on experience and relating to a terrible concrete case. One wonders, especially today, whether politicians and public opinion have learned this lesson. Unfortunately, it would seem not.

The time when Hoover and Roosevelt were in the White House was a continuum: Roosevelt's innovations were expansions or intensifications of Hoover's measures. With Roosevelt's New Deal, executive power over social and political life steadily grew. As Garet Garrett notes, in 1938, the New Deal, led by an elite of revolutionary intellectuals, concentrated political and economic power in the executive. "The ultimate power of initiative" passed from private enterprise to government, "which became the great capitalist and enterpriser" (Garrett, 1953, p. 31).

4 Rothbard and the Economic and Social History of the Progressive Era

Among Rothbard's posthumous works, special attention should be paid to *The Progressive Era*, released in 2017, thanks to the Ludwig von Mises Institute, and edited by Patrick Newman (Rothbard, 2017). The idea for the volume was conceived during the 1970s, at the time of Rothbard's involvement with the Cato Institute. Unfortunately, the book remained unfinished, but the author completed it by publishing a series of essays that were published between the 80s and 90s. The editor of *The Progressive Era* took charge of adding these essays to the text, thus completing the volume and enriching it with notes where missing. It is a fundamental text that can be considered the premise of *The Great Depression*, since in the Progressive Era, we find the first traces of those policies that, following the economic crisis and the first interventionist measures of President Hoover, would pave the way for Roosevelt's New Deal. It is therefore a question of tracing the origins of a sea change in American economic policy. As Rothbard himself explains in his preface,

> The aim of this proposed book is to trace the origins of the current welfare-warfare state in America, in what is loosely called "The Progressive Period," from approximately the mid-1890s to the mid-1920s. Briefly, the thesis is that the rapid upsurge of statism in this period was propelled by a coalition of two broad groups: (a) certain big business groups, anxious to replace a roughly *laissez-faire* economy by a new form of mercantilism, cartelized and controlled and subsidized by a strong government under their influence and control; and (b) newly burgeoning groups of intellectuals, technocrats, and professionals: economists, writers, engineers, planners, physicians, etc., anxious for power and lucrative employment at the hands of the State. Since America had been born in an antimonopoly tradition, it became important to put over the new system of cartelization as a "progressive" curbing of big business by a humanitarian government; intellectuals were relied on for this selling job. These two groups were inspired by Bismarck's creation of a monopolized welfare warfare state in Prussia and Germany. (Rothbard, 2017, p. 37)

The typical economic system of the ancien régime was mercantilism with forms of protectionism and subsidies that favored certain commercial sectors and special interests, the goal being more exports and fewer imports. With the birth of Adam Smith's political economy, followed by the industrial revolution in England and the American colonies in the seventeenth and eighteenth centuries, there were substantial changes in the direction of governments limited in powers and functions and an economic system of laissez-faire that could be controlled directly by the people. Why, then, Rothbard asks in the volume, this reversal of course with the Progressive Era? Why this return of statism and regulation of many economic sectors? It was a veritable explosion of statism that could be explained by an alliance between big business, big governments, intellectual elites, and trade unions.

Rothbard's thesis is that large industrialists and financiers had previously sought to create cartels and monopolies in the late-nineteenth and early-twentieth centuries. Their attempts, however, failed due to external pressure from business rivals entering the market by lowering prices. So it was that big business decided to turn to government regulation to create cartels that would prevent various forms of competition, preventing new manufacturers from entering different markets. The government, for its part, by regulating the economy to ally itself with big business, would increase its power. But this return to the past in new forms, which would have been to the detriment of the public, could not simply be imposed on the American population, accustomed as it was to the principles of laissez-faire and the benefits they brought in terms of costs and quality of products and services. The new course was, in a sense, sold to the public, raising a new caste of collectivist intellectuals, many of whom had obtained their PhDs in Germany and appreciated Bismarck's socialist policies. The new intellectuals, who were apologists for government interests, were able to convince the public that to increase the welfare of the community and remedy many social ills, a stronger and interventionist government—a big government—was needed to control without constraints or restrictions a capitalism that was considered responsible for society's many problems and inequalities. In return for their work of convincing the public, the intellectuals would receive many benefits from the government: they would become professional intellectuals and obtain well-paid jobs as planners and administrators of the entire apparatus.

Ultimately, it was the big businessmen themselves who ceased to be the advocates of laissez-faire, and it was they who were first interested in developing government rules to prevent others from entering the market by creating cartels and thereby decreasing supply and raising prices. This is clearly opposed to the classic narrative that regulations were introduced for the benefit of the population but also to the idea that the bureaucracy, interested in increasing its power through the various government agencies, is at the center of the initiative. Rothbard, in fact, combines the interests of big business and those of bureaucracy in his original analysis of the Progressive Era. He is interested in getting to the bottom of and understanding the different motivations of special interests that led to the lobbying that in turn led to the new government regulation. Rothbard, moreover, being a great connoisseur of the theory of elites, understood that it was not the great majority of voters or public opinion that controlled the work of legislators but small interest groups well rooted in society—that is, financial, industrial, and political elites able to control government agenda, as well as government officials and bureaucrats who often have deep social, cultural, and even familial ties to the entire community of businessmen and industrialists. The basic thesis, supported by Rothbard, is that the American welfare-warfare state has matured and grown from its first steps in the Progressive Era.

How did this begin? The first large-scale industry in America that tried to form cartels and limit competition was the railroads. When its attempt failed, the government stepped in to regulate it. In the 1850s, the American railroads began their "epic story of rapid and remarkable growth" (Rothbard, 2017, p. 41).

The first four major transcontinental railroads to be built were Central Pacific, Southern Pacific, Union Pacific, and Northern Pacific. Until the late 1880s, there was healthy competition in this industry that changed the face of the United States and the lifestyle of Americans. At one point, the main managers of the railway sector tried to agree to make cartels, raise prices, and eliminate potential competitors in the sector. If, in the beginning, the general public welcomed the increase in prices as a topic of conversation, discontent gradually grew, and finally the cartels could not withstand the pressure of new competitors entering the railway sector with lower prices. At that point, it was clear that only government obligation could support a cartel policy, and so the men of the big railway business turned to the government, which was supposed to protect the railways from speculators willing to compete without rules (Rothbard, 2017, pp. 67–69). In 1884, Democrat Grover Cleveland won the presidency. He had always been in favor of laissez-faire, but he had worked extensively in the railroad industry and did not oppose the passage of the Interstates Commerce Act, following which the Inter-State Commerce Railway Association cartel was established. Theodore Roosevelt's presidency continued along the path it had taken, further strengthening protectionist policy toward the railroads. The rail sector had to be protected from competition and bad and dishonest competitors.

The temptation to establish cartels and monopolies, restrict production, and raise prices began to hit one industrial sector after another. The first major attempt to establish a single large industry, and consequently a monopoly, occurred in the oil sector by John D. Rockefeller, who within a few years incorporated the various emerging refineries into the Standard Oil Company in Ohio, the largest refinery in the world (Rothbard, 2017, p. 94). In 1879, Rockefeller was responsible for nearly 90% of America's oil refining capacity. Despite its quasi-monopoly position, Standard Oil was never able to limit production and raise prices. The price of kerosene—the main oil product of that period—in fact fell in that decade as oil extraction increased. Standard Oil's position began to falter, and Rockefeller had to abandon his monopolistic aims. Meanwhile, new companies such as the Texas Company and Gulf Oil emerged. Similarly, other sectors—such as iron, steel, agriculture, and sugar—tried to reach agreements and create cartels; but without state support, they failed. So it was that big businessmen from the beginning of the twentieth century increasingly turned to the federal government for help. Rothbard reiterates that federal intervention was not intended to rein in the free market for the benefit of citizens or consumers but was conceived and implemented under pressure from big business. It was a deliberate attempt to flood the economy with subsidies and give businesses monopolistic positions (Rothbard, 2010, pp. 31–32).

A distinctively American culture and spirit helped create a positive and welcoming attitude toward the Progressive Era. A kind of spiritual movement in itself, the Progressive Era found its leaders and followers among ministers of worship, social workers, intellectuals, and professional philanthropists, who with great Christian zeal were convinced that they had to rebuild America in the image of God and that humanity had as its task the creation of the kingdom of God on earth. Protestant pietism from the mid-nineteenth century until the beginning of the twentieth century, however, underwent a gradual process of secularization. The need to rely on the government to eliminate sin from a society that was to be made in the image of God became increasingly evident. Thus was born the powerful movement of the Social Gospel, which, starting in Chicago and the local realities of Wisconsin, branched out and took root in most of the United States to become an ally of the government with the task of correcting, organizing, and eventually planning a perfect society (Rothbard, 2017, pp. 333–334). The American welfare state has its roots in the Social Gospel movement, which supported state intervention both in the personal sphere—supporting temperance and the fight against alcohol—and in the economic sphere. It was therefore a powerful supporter of the Republican Party against the Democratic Party, in favor of personal and economic freedom.

When Theodore Roosevelt became president in 1901, he selected three advisers, economists in favor of government-regulated cartelization of business and opposed to laissez-faire: Edwin A. Seligman, a professor at Columbia University from a prominent banking family; Arthur Twining Hadrey, president of Yale; and Jeremiah W. Jenks from Cornell University and chief adviser to the US Industrial Commission, whose task was to control trusts. The three new advisers all came from what Rothbard calls the "new school" in economics, which a decade earlier had repudiated the idea of the free market in favor of increasing state control of the economy and had advocated the establishment of the Interstate Commerce Commission in 1887. At this point, surrounded by such advisers, Roosevelt became increasingly determined to regulate cartels, trusts, and corporations in general, establishing obligations, taxes, and licensing for various activities. Cartels and capital accumulation were perfectly legitimate in Roosevelt's view, but government regulation and control were necessary to prevent them from happening in a predatory manner (Rothbard, 2017, p. 211). "At about the same time the nation acquired its first progressive President Theodore Roosevelt, various big business leaders decided to organize on behalf of the new concept, one which has in recent years been termed 'corporate liberalism'. The nation was to be guided into the new path of a strong State, expanding, regulating, and governing all in behalf of a tripartite coalition led by Big Business, by means of Big Government, and creating Big Unionism as junior partner" (Rothbard, 2017, p. 273).

Based on the contents and theses illustrated in *The Progressive Era*, it is evident that, although the volume was published posthumously in 2017, it expresses the logical premises of *The Great Depression*, published in 1963. It contains, in fact, the background and preconditions that led to several moments of economic crisis and eventually to the Great Depression itself, as well as to what Rothbard called Herbert Hoover's New Deal.

5 A New Analysis of Taxes and Public Spending: What Would a World Without it be Like?

Power and Market is defined by Nicola Iannello as "a pivotal point" (Iannello, 2017, p. 7) in Rothbard's intellectual production. In fact, it is precisely in this volume that Rothbard, for the first time, fully lays out the hypothesis of a society completely devoid of coercion—that is, a society in which even the services of protection against aggression and the administration of justice are not provided by a state monopoly but are offered by the market, as with any other good or service. The idea of a monopoly on the exercise of force and the administration of justice in a given territory is rejected, and Rothbard instead puts forward the hypothesis of a plurality of protection agencies acting in reciprocal competition on the same territory and from which individuals could freely choose to receive protection and judicial administration. Justice would be administered by judges—that is, private professionals—who would apply a legal code based on the "axiom of nonaggression," the true cornerstone of Rothbard's political-philosophical construction. According to this axiom, no one—not even the state—can be attacked in person and property. Rothbard criticizes economists for believing that the market should be maintained through the invasive actions of government institutions. Instead, he promotes a free society in which force is used only to defend against attacks on the person or property of others. "This would imply the complete absence of a State apparatus or government; for the State, unlike all other persons and institutions in society, acquires its revenue, not by exchanges freely contracted, but by a system of unilateral coercion called 'taxation.' … Defense services, like all other services, would be marketable and marketable only" (Rothbard, 1970, p. 2).

It is certainly true that *Power and Market* represents a turning point in Rothbard's production, but in reality, he had been reflecting on questions of political philosophy and political theory for many years. It has already been noted that Rothbard, in an unpublished 1954 paper—"The Concepts 'Rational' and 'Irrational'"—detaches himself from Mises and claims the possibility of a rational foundation of ethics, rejecting the nonavalutative approach to the defense of freedom (Rothbard, 1954, forthcoming). Moreover, while we find in *Power and Market* the exposition of the Rothbardian project of a society without a state or coercion, it should be noted that Rothbard wrote an unpublished essay in December 1958 entitled "On Gustave de Molinari" (Rothbard, 1958, forthcoming). At the time, he hoped that de Molinari's work would be translated into English and published in the United States. He shows great admiration for an essay presented by de Molinari, which will be published in the United States in 1977 (De Molinari, 1977).

before the Society of Political Economy calling for an extension of the private, competitive system to the police function. This article was published

> in the *Journal des Économistes* in 1849, under the title "De la Production de la Sécurité." Molinari thus arrived at the first expression of what we may perhaps call anarcho-capitalism purely from [the] economic rather than from the political realm. In short, he reasoned: a free competition suppl [ies] consumers with the most efficient service, and monopoly was always bad in all other goods and services, why should this not apply to the service of defense. (Rothbard, 1958, forthcoming)

In *An Austrian Perspective on the History of Economic Thought*, published posthumously, de Molinari is again defined as the first anarchocapitalist (Rothbard, 1995, pp. 453–455). The 1963 paper "Toward a Strategy for Libertarians" seems to be a first draft—although it is not identical—of the final chapter of *The Ethics of Liberty*, published in 1982 (Rothbard, 1963, forthcoming). Even in this paper, we already find an anarchocapitalist Rothbard. All this is to highlight that Rothbard had long since brought his theory and political philosophy to maturity. *Power and Market* combines economics and anti-statism, but at a certain point in his reasoning, Rothbard makes a statement that seems to reveal some doubt: "The worst that could possibly happen would be for the State to be reestablished. And since the State is what we have *now*, any experimentation with a stateless society would have nothing to lose and everything to gain" (Rothbard, 1970, p. 9). Such a statement projects us toward a future uncertainty found in the discourse of *The Ethics of Liberty* concerning the strategy of moving from the current world to the future stateless society. We are still far from that deep maturation found later in *Nations by Consent: Decomposing the Nation State*—written shortly before his death—in which Rothbard seems to discover a different approach to de-statization.

In *Power and Market*, Rothbard examines the ways an attacker can intervene in the market. In the first type of intervention, an aggressor commands an individual to perform or not perform certain actions that involve only the individual in question and his property. This is autistic intervention, a limitation of a person's actions, such as the freedom to exercise a religion, or of the use that the person can make of his property, with no other people involved. Binary intervention occurs when the aggressor imposes a hegemony over the victim—for example, by forcing the victim to make an exchange or to give him part of his property. Examples of binary intervention are banditry, taxes, and compulsory conscription, according to Rothbard. Finally, triangular intervention is when the aggressor imposes or prohibits an exchange between two subjects. In this way, a hegemonic relationship is created by the aggressor over the potential or actual participants in the exchange. Rothbard notes that economists have recognized only the triangular type of intervention as market intervention and interference. In a free market, people participate in an exchange only if they benefit from it. Any intervention in that exchange can only increase utility for the aggressor and decrease it for those who undergo the intervention.

Against this, one could argue that since intervention takes place in democracies, it is voluntary and supported by the majority of the people. But it is very difficult to argue that those in the minority, or who did not vote at all, can support government intervention or that citizens can support a state from apathy or as the lesser of two evils. When government policies fail, politicians will not necessarily suffer a loss of votes, because voters may be unable to identify the causes of failure. The government, therefore, has mechanisms at hand to continue its inefficient choices. On the market, inept entrepreneurs unable to best serve consumers are doomed to failure, but a politician can win elections by appealing to voters with skillful demagoguery. According to Rothbard, Franz Oppenheimer offers one of the best analyses of the distinction between state and market. He identified two essential ways of obtaining the means of subsistence: (1) voluntary production and exchange; and (2) violent expropriation of another's property. Oppenheimer defines the first method as "the economic means" and the second as "the political means" (Rothbard, 1970, pp. 11–12; Oppenheimer, 1914).

The triangular intervention, as already mentioned, occurs when the aggressor imposes, prohibits, or somehow interferes in an exchange between two subjects. There are several examples of triangular intervention. A typical intervention of this type is price control. If the intervention fixes a maximum price above which a product may not be sold, the immediate effect is scarcity as the quantity of demand exceeds supply, which in turn leads to rationing, long lines to obtain certain goods, and favoritism for some consumers and discrimination against others, all of which is evidently unwelcome to the government in power. If the intervener sets a minimum price below which a product may not be sold, the result is that supply exceeds demand for the good in question. A typical example of such a situation is mass unemployment resulting from laws establishing the minimum wage.

Another type of triangular intervention is the prohibition of the production and sale of a given product. The consequence of prohibition will be the emergence of a black market, because the product in question will have to be sold outside legal channels. There will therefore be an increase in prices, because the supply will be more limited and the producer will have to compensate for the risk of violating the law. Pressure to reestablish the market, however, will be inevitable even if the product offered is of the worst quality, because the organization of the market will be less efficient. There may also be various degrees of prohibition—as when the government grants monopoly privileges by imposing cartels to help struggling companies at the expense of the consumer. Another example is the licensing system, which allows only certain groups to produce certain goods or services, with the apparent aim of guaranteeing better quality to consumers. All this, however, eliminates the possibility of lowering the prices of goods and services.

Another clear case of triangular intervention is the imposition of tariffs on international products or duties, which are meant to protect producers within a country. This intervention harms local consumers by raising prices, as well as foreign producers and domestic exporters in other sectors. Immigration restrictions are also a triangular intervention that distorts costs in the labor market. Employers tend to shift production from high-wage to low-wage areas, while workers gravitate toward higher-wage areas. This dynamic tends to equalize wage rates for the same type of productive work across different locations. Barriers to immigration instead confer gains at the expense of foreign workers, raise prices for consumers, and contribute to hostility between nations. Rothbard also sees child labor laws that reduce forced unemployment as benefiting older workers while disadvantaging poor families with children. "Child labor laws, by restricting the supply of labor, lower the production of the economy and hence tend to reduce the standard of living of everyone in the society" (Rothbard, 1970, p. 66). Compulsory schooling laws, by forcing children up to a certain age to remain in state schools, protect older workers from competition and deprive children and their parents of the freedom to choose another type of activity. Finally, unemployment benefits are yet another form of triangular intervention. These benefits subsidize the unemployment that trade unions and the minimum wage cause, preventing unemployed workers from breaking union solidarity. The mass of potential competitors to the trade unions are thereby excluded from the labor market, allowing trade union policies to continue. And of course, unemployment benefits are financed by taxpayers (Rothbard, 1970, pp. 66–68).

Environmental protection and environmental protection laws are very popular today. Rothbard already considered this topic in *Power and Market* as a triangular intervention by the state. Government measures aimed at limiting the use of nonrenewable resources go against individuals' time preferences and force owners to invest in renewable natural resources—that is, current production is limited to a supposed advantage in future production. Nonrenewable resources are consumed in the present, but, it is said, one should think about future generations. Owners are also supposed to conserve renewable resources, such as trees, even if it is more profitable to use them in other forms of production. People's time preferences are thereby altered, forcing them to allocate resources so that they invest more in future consumption. "In short, the State decides that the present generation must be made to allocate its resources more to the future than it wishes to do; for this service the State is held up as being 'farseeing,' compared to 'shortsighted' free individuals" (Rothbard, 1970, p. 77). A balance should be struck between present and future production. Why do the needs of the current generation count for so little? It is very likely that future generations will be richer than the current ones, so why should present generations bear a greater burden? Among other things, after a certain number of years, the future will become the present, but the time preferences of the present will still have to be sacrificed. Owners decide the temporal structure of the allocation of factors of production according to the expected income that their resources will procure in the present. They will therefore tend to increase the value of resources rather than decrease it in a shortsighted way. A lower time preference will lead to greater investment in future consumer goods, and this will result in greater protection of natural resources, without any state intervention. Rothbard laments environmentalists' total lack of familiarity with economic theory. Many assume that entrepreneurs have no foresight and will waste their resources, finding themselves without any property tomorrow. Is it possible for those who are directly concerned and understand their own circumstances to make worse predictions than a centralized bureaucrat? Moreover, since technology is not something fixed in time, technological knowledge develops and usable resources multiply. Rich countries, notes Johann Norberg, have found solutions to many environmental problems. Industrialization and wealth creation allow poor countries to deal with serious environmental and pollution problems. "What is important is that our climate policies don't hurt our ability to create more wealth and better technologies and to bring power to the world's poor. That would be a case of killing the patient to cure the disease" (Norberg, 2016, p. 90). Why does Rothbard consider environmental interventions to be "triangular" intrusions in the economy and the market? America was one of the first countries to introduce, through public ownership, such regulations. Logically, Rothbard explains there would be no government-owned public domain in a free market. A clear example of how these policies can be counterproductive can be seen in the government's prohibition against fencing the vast pastures of the American West during the nineteenth century, which forced ranchers to rely on open-range grazing. The result was overexploitation and premature depletion of pastures. Why, then, would anyone support environmental legislation? Environmental protection laws limit production—that is, the use of a resource—and consequently generate a monopoly privilege, which leads to a price restriction for the owners of that resource. "Conservation laws, on the other hand, serve to cartelize a land factor and absolutely restrict production, thereby helping to insure permanent (and continuing) monopoly gains for the owners … . Conservation laws, therefore, must also be looked upon as grants of monopolistic privilege" (Rothbard, 1970, p. 83). The American forest protection policy, for example, sets restrictionist prices and confers monopoly advantages over the remaining land in use. That is why when Theodore Roosevelt adopted the first policies for the protection of forests, the major users of timber understood and supported the initiative, simply because they realized the great advantages they would gain from forests being protected. Government policies that put forest takeover out of business only increased the timber of large landowners (Rothbard, 1970, p. 86).

Finally, patenting is another government policy that can be analyzed through the perspective of triangular intervention. This is the state's granting of monopoly privilege to the discoverers of new inventions. Rothbard points out that this is not a legitimate form of ownership but a limitation of others' ability to use their property. The argument in favor of patents is that they would stimulate research and development, but this claim is based on the completely arbitrary assumption that there would not be enough research in a free market.

In *Man, Economy, and State*, Rothbard argues that no monopoly can arise from the market, and in *Power and Market*, he shows how all monopoly positions are the result of triangular government interventions. In the last chapters of *Power and Market*, Rothbard deals with the typical binary intervention of taxation. The state bases its survival on taxation, and society is divided between tax consumers and tax payers. Tax consumers—that is, politicians, bureaucrats of various kinds, and state-subsidized citizens—benefit from taxation while others foot the bill. Rothbard, contrary to the Keynesian approach, immediately clarifies as follows: Any expenditure by the state is consumption and never investment, since the state does not produce wealth but limits itself to distorting the allocation of resources by subtracting them from production. All sales tax is income tax, and income taxes reduce people's purchasing power and represent a disincentive to earn. Income taxes reduce both consumption and the propensity to save, negatively affecting quality of life and economic growth. It is, however, intuitive that income taxes are not conducive to saving at all, since individuals tend to save for future consumption, and tend to encourage undeclared work. Taxes on wages are not passed on to the entrepreneur; instead, the employer's social security contributions are subtracted from the employee's salary. Taxes on savings, therefore, are rightly accused of being a double taxation, because they tax capital that has already suffered taxation. Along with inheritance taxes, these taxes on income tend to destroy capital, machinery, and inherited companies. Gift taxes, just like inheritance taxes, tend to impoverish voluntary philanthropy and family ties. So-called taxes on excess profits are nothing more than punishments for the most successful companies. Progressive taxation, in addition to discouraging work and reducing savings, is theft from both rich and poor.

Bureaucrats and, in general, government agents spend taxpayers' money to achieve their own ends; therefore, any government spending is consumption and not investment. No service provided by the state can be free, due to the scarcity of resources involved. The myth of free public services is a myth because citizens pay much more in taxes than they would pay private individuals offering the same services and because individuals are forced to pay even for services they may not be interested in. It is literally impossible for the state to manage production on an entrepreneurial basis, because it obtains its funding through coercion, which leads to the distortion of incentive and makes it impossible for public personnel to serve and satisfy the wishes of consumers. Even if a public enterprise competed with private individuals, there would still be a distortion caused by the original sin of having started the business with the coercion of taxation. Ultimately, any such company should be completely privatized.

What about the theory of democracy typical of the school of public choice, according to which the process that takes place in the market is similar to what happens in the political arena? After all, citizens vote for public policies that include taxation, for which they receive services in exchange. In 1962, James Buchanan and Gordon Tullock, starting from the premises of methodological individualism, addressed the problem of the rational choice of the individual at the time of the foundation of a political community (Buchanan and Tullock, 2004). *The Calculus of Consent* is in the tradition of classical liberalism, and the authors argue that the mechanism of voting in the political arena is of the same nature as consumer choice in the market. In Rothbard's view, this analogy is not tenable. Its premise is that coercion is inherent in public choices. The very term *common will* would be intrinsically contradictory when referring to individuals who are members of a community. Political decisions, as Bruno Leoni also argued, "always imply an element that is not compatible with individual freedom, and therefore not compatible with a true representation of the will of those people whose choice has possibly been rejected in the decision adopted" (Leoni, 2005, p. 78). The majority rule would not be compatible with individual freedom of choice. Decision-making should always be approached from a perspective of methodological individualism. But the political decision is usually a group decision—that is, a decision by which the individualistic perspective is altered, a single decision by some that must apply to the whole group. In a representative political system, the dissenting minority is subject to the decisions of the majority. Where it is not possible to reach a unanimous decision, the only logical tool for reaching group decisions is coercion. There are also those who wonder to what extent the dissenting minority is obligated to submit to the will of the majority (Raico, 2012, p. 283). The issue had already been raised by Gustave de Molinari, who strenuously rejected the idea that property owners should passively adhere to the confiscatory measures of a democratic majority (de Molinari, 1977).

But if politics is the realm of collective choice, then the attempt by proponents of the school of public choice to equate individuals who make choices in the market with voters in the political arena is unfounded (Black, 1950, pp. 506–511). As long as political choices are considered a set of collective choices, economics and politics must be considered profoundly different. While individuals always get something in return for their economic choices, voters in the minority get nothing in return for their vote. While the market is a place of voluntary interactions, the democratic legal order produces aggression and casualties because collective decisions are imposed against the will of a part of the social body and at its expense. In this regard, it is necessary to recall Mises's thesis that in exchange relations the individual is never a member of a dissenting minority, as is always the case in representative political systems. As Mises notes, "in the political democracy only the votes cast for the majority candidate or the majority plan are effective in shaping the course of affairs. The vote polled by the minority do not directly influence politics. But on the market no vote is cast in vain" (Mises, 1998, p. 271). If coercion cannot be eliminated from collective choices, then juxtaposition is impossible.

Power and Market delves deep into the democratic topic. Rothbard had begun to reflect on this issue well before 1970. In an unpublished paper from 1959, he questions a classic argument that is usually brought to defend democracy—namely that the democratic process allows for peaceful changes of government (Rothbard, 1959, forthcoming). Much of this analysis will be found later in *Power and Market*. "Perhaps the leading argument for democracy is that it substitutes 'ballots for bullets': that it replaces the inconvenient and disruptive processes of violent change by peaceful changes expressing the majority will. Some democrats have defined democracy as majority rule, while others have placed on this rule the limitation that minorities must themselves be left free to try to become a majority" (Rothbard, 1959, forthcoming). Although this is considered one of the most persuasive arguments, in Rothbard's view, it has not been analyzed or deepened to any great extent. The argument is that it is much better to let the majority exercise its right to govern peacefully, as in a democracy, than to force the majority to periodically overthrow the government through revolutions and riots. But, Rothbard notes there is an internal contradiction here that has not yet been investigated. The idea that ballot papers have replaced bullets is based on the assumption that the result of a peaceful democratic election must be the same as a violent revolution (Rothbard, 1959, forthcoming). Here, we have a criterion by which to evaluate the democratic process: Does it in reality have the same effects as a civil war? Rothbard applies this criterion to the democratic principle of "one man, one vote." In the first place, physical strength is not distributed equally: the sick, women, and the elderly would not prevail in a physical confrontation, which means they could be deprived of the right to vote. Moreover, those who have received military training to become more competent fighters, such as soldiers and policemen, might be given special privileges (Rothbard, 1959, forthcoming).

There is another aspect that the government's "peaceful change" argument completely ignores: the differences in intensity of interest in political issues and elections in general. There are completely apathetic individuals who might go to the polls just for the sake of a pleasant walk. But it is not certain that everyone who votes would also be eager to fight in the streets to defend their political side. Some people are interested in elections, and others are not. Here, too, the argument about replacing bullets with ballots does not hold water (Rothbard, 1959, forthcoming). Going to vote is extremely easy. One could institute, as Rothbard proposes, a *poll tax*—not so high as to discourage those who are genuinely interested but sufficient to keep away the apathetic (Rothbard, 1959, forthcoming). In his 1959 paper, Rothbard concludes that the argument of a "peaceful change" of government in support of democracy should be abandoned and that "the existing democracies could certainly never be justified by the argument" (Rothbard, 1959, forthcoming).

Power and Market further explores the theme of democracy. First, Rothbard considers the scenario in which an overwhelming majority votes for a dictator. If a democracy could vote against its very existence, then it would be nothing more than "a *transition* to a nondemocratic form of government" (Rothbard, 1970, p. 234). In a socialist system, then, democracy is not even conceivable. "The ruling party, owning all means of production, will have the complete decision … not to speak of its economic power over all the individual leaders and members of the opposition" (Rothbard, 1970, p. 235). On the other hand, the corruption in socialist countries is well known (see Freedom House data). No one believes any longer that the majority is always right and always decides for the best—as an expression of an ambiguous and general Rousseauian will—especially considering the experiences of the twentieth century. Moreover, in a very original way, Rothbard relates democracy to the right of secession: "For if someone contends that the majority in Country X should govern that country, then it could be argued with equal validity that the majority of a certain district within Country X should be allowed to govern *itself* and secede from the larger country, and this subdividing process can logically proceed down to the village block, the apartment house, and, finally, each individual, thus marking the end of all democratic government through reduction to individual self government" (Rothbard, 1970, p. 237). But if such a right of secession is denied, then the advocate of democracy falls into contradiction. Mises, in

Liberalism, argues that the constitution of a country should provide for the right to secession (Mises, 2005, p. 79).

Rothbard ultimately believes that "the arguments for democracy are thus shown to be a maze of fallacy and contradiction" (Rothbard, 1970, p. 245). But his suggestion is not simply to abandon or reduce democracy but to see it as a tool or means to achieve other ends. "Democracy, after all, is simply a method of choosing governors and issues, and it is not so surprising that it might have value largely to the extent that it serves as a *means* to other political ends" (Rothbard, 1970, p. 245). While recognizing in democracy a jumble of contradictions, Rothbard is not prepared to abandon the hope that it is precisely through democratic consultation that a libertarian society could be established. "The libertarian might thus consider democracy as a useful way of protecting people against government or of advancing individual liberty" (Rothbard, 1970, p. 245). But here too there are contradictions. If the limits and guarantees of individual liberty are entrusted to an organ of the government itself, these limits will be continuously weakened. This was highlighted by John C. Calhoun in *Disquisition on Government,* and Hayek himself, as we have seen, toward the end of his career expressed his disillusionment with constitutionalism as a means of protecting individual liberties and protecting against government (Calhoun, 1851).

Despite Rothbard's many criticisms toward and perplexities about democracy, Rothbard has not theorized a radical assimilation between democracy and socialist drift, nor does he seem willing to simply abandon the democratic process. The task of elaborating the most radical and irreverent critique of democracy, as we will see later, will fall to his pupil Hans-Hermann Hoppe.

Perhaps one of the most original and visionary aspects of Rothbardian analysis is his prediction of what is now called web democracy. Already in 1970, he wrote that "modern technology *does* make it possible to have direct democracy. Certainly, each man could easily vote on issues several times per week by recording his choice on a device attached to his television set. This would not be difficult to achieve" (Rothbard, 1970, p. 238). But in such a direct democracy, Rothbard sees many flaws. The first problem is that the vast majority of voters will not be equipped with the specific knowledge and skills to express themselves on complex issues. Rothbard also has doubts about whether the majority even have sufficient powers to elect representatives. People may not know the candidates, know absolutely nothing, or be influenced by the mass media.

Having raised this question in 1970, before the internet existed, leads to some pressing reflections. Web democracy would seem today to make possible Rousseau's popular sovereignty without intermediation—the true sovereignty of the people (Grilli di Cortona and Modugno, 2020, pp. 49–52). Recent developments in technology allow for previously unknown possibilities, such as online platforms to enable direct civic participation and consultation for a wide range of issues. The fascination of direct democracy is increasingly fueled by new technologies and the development of a new network ideology (Grilli di Cortona and Modugno, 2020, pp. 46–49). The impact of new mass media, Internet, and social media on the formation of public opinion has strongly undermined representative democracy. In this ideological struggle between the few in power and the many outside power, a populist democracy has been growing. This is not so much a crisis of democracy as it is a crisis in democracy and a deterioration of democratic quality, which is the theme of Nadia Urbinati's *Me the People: How Populism Transforms Democracy* (Urbinati, 2019). Leonardo Morlino and Ernesto Raniolo describe what happens when in a democracy in economic crisis the people of the resistance become the majority in government and are engaged in managing public affairs—"a context of political culture where the majority of citizens believe that 'democracy must distribute' resources and benefits and where consequently the goal of participation is to encourage a greater response from government institutions" (Morlino and Raniolo, 2018, p. 189). The next step in web democracy is social media democracy, social media now being the most important mass media. This kind of democracy leads to deadlocks in which political leaders increasingly behave like *followers* trying to gain public support and at the same time leaders trying to manipulate the masses through new tools for collecting and analyzing data from the network. The masses themselves are, in turn, able to direct the rulers, who find themselves having to indulge the masses in order not to lose consensus. At the same time, public opinion becomes emotional and is as easily changeable as emotions.

One should not forget Jacob L. Talmon's always timely warning from his 1952 book *The Origins of Totalitarian Democracy*, in which he wondered what had led to the totalitarianisms of the twentieth century. "Modern totalitarian democracy is a dictatorship resting on popular enthusiasm, and is thus completely different from absolute power wielded by a divine-right King, or by a usurping tyrant. In so far as it is a dictatorship based on ideology and the enthusiasm of the masses, it is the outcome, as will be shown, of the synthesis between the eighteenth-century idea of the natural order and the Rousseauist idea of popular fulfillment and self-expression" (Talmon, 1952, p. 6). And about direct democracy, he writes, "Ultimately the Legislature would have only the right to initiate legislation, but not to decide upon it ... . But such plebiscitary, direct democracy is ... the preliminary of dictatorship or dictatorship in disguise. It is an invitation to a totalitarian party in opposition to whip up agitation, to 'organize' the discontent or the will of the people, by engineering mass petitions, manifestations, and pressure from below; and an encouragement to a totalitarian party in power to engineer referenda mid mass resolutions of support" (Talmon, 1952, pp. 206–207). But are we really willing to do without mediation in a mass society like ours? Are we willing to entrust public choices to a populist network, where everyone thinks that the most urgent problems are within everyone's reach? It is a short step from here to illiberal plebiscitarianism.

References

Bazzichi, O. (2003). *Alle radici del capitalismo: Medioevo e scienza economica.* Effatà.

Black, D. (1950). The unity of political and economic science. *Economic Journal, 239*(60), 506–514.

Block, W., Geoffrey, B., & Elzinga, K. (Eds.). (1985). *Morality of the market: Religious and economic perspectives.* Fraser Institute.

Buchanan, J., & Tullock, G. (2004). *The calculus of consent: Logical foundations of constitutional democracy.* Liberty Fund, Original work published 1962.

Calhoun, J. C. (1851), *A disquisition on government.* A. S. Johnston.

de Molinari, G. (1977). *On the production of security.* Center for Libertarian Studies, Original work published 1849.

de Roover, R. (1955). Scholastic economics: Survival and lasting influence from the sixteenth century to adam smith. *Quarterly Journal of Economics, 69*(2), 161–190.

de Roover, R. (1967). *San Bernardino of Siena and Sant'Antonino of Florence: The two great economic thinkers of the middle ages.* Harvard Graduate School of Business Administration.

Garrett, G. (1953). The Revolution was. In *The People's Pottage.* Caxton.

Gordon, D. (1993). *The philosophical origins of Austrian economics.* Ludwig von Mises Institute.

Gordon, D. (2004). Le implicazioni etiche e politiche della scuola austriaca di economia. In D. Gordon & R. A. Modugno (Eds.), *Individualismo metodologico: dalla Scuola austriaca all'anarcocapitalismo*. Luiss University Press.

Grice-Hutchinson, M. (2009). *The School of Salamanca: readings in Spanish Monetary Theory 1544–1605*. Ludwig von Mises Institute, Original work published 1952.

Grilli Di Cortona, P., & Modugno, R. A. (2020). *Le trame della democrazia: Riflessioni tra politologia e storia del pensiero politico*. Rubbettino.

Iannello, N. (2017). La scienza politica di un economista: Scambio e potere secondo Murray N. Rothbard. In M. N. Rothbard (Ed.), Introduzione to *Potere e mercato: lo Stato e l'economia*. IBL Libri.

Kauder, E. (1953a). Genesis of the marginal utility theory: From aristotle to the end of the eighteenth century. *Economic Journal, 63*(251), 638–650.

Kauder, E. (1953b). Retarded acceptance of the marginal utility theory. *Quarterly Journal of Economics 67*(4), 564–575.

Leoni, B. (2005). *Freedom and the Law*. Liberty Fund, Original work published 1963.

Mises, L. V. (1998). *Human action: A treatise on economics*. Ludwig von Mises Institute, Original work published 1949.

Mises, L. V. (2005). *Liberalism: The classical tradition*. Liberty Fund, Original work published 1927.

Morlino, L., & Raniolo, F. (2018). *Come la crisi economica cambia la democrazia: Tra insoddisfazione e protesta*. Il Mulino.

Norberg, J. (2016). *Progress: Ten reasons to look forward to the future*. Oneworld.

Nuccio, O. (1995). *La civiltà italiana nella formazione della scienza economica*. Etas Libri.

Oppenheimer, F. (1914). *The State: Its history and development viewed sociologically*. Vanguard.

Raico, R. (2012). *Classical liberalism and the Austrian school*. Ludwig von Mises Institute.

Raimondo, J. (2000). *An enemy of the state: The life of Murray N Rothbard*. Prometheus.

Rothbard, M. M. (Forthcoming). The logical consequences of the 'peaceful change' argument for democracy," February 1959. In R. A. Modugno (Ed.), *Murray Rothbard on politics, philosophy, and history: A selection from his papers*. Ludwig von Mises Institute.

Rothbard, M. N. (1957b). In defense of 'extreme apriorism'. *Southern Economic Journal 23* (3), 314–320.

Rothbard, M. N. (1962). *Man, economy and State: A treatise on economic principles*. Van Nostrand.

Rothbard, M. N. (Forthcoming). Toward a strategy for libertarians. Summer 1963. In R. A. Modugno (Ed.), *Murray Rothbard on politics, philosophy, and history: A selection from his papers.* Ludwig von Mises Institute.
Rothbard, M. N. (1963). *America's great depression.* Van Nostrand.
Rothbard, M. N. (1970). *Power and market: Government and the economy.* Institute for Humane Studies.
Rothbard, M. N. (1976). New light on the Prehistory of the Austrian school. In E. G. Dolan (Ed.), *The foundations of modern Austrian economics.* Sheed and Ward.
Rothbard, M. N. (1995). *An Austrian perspective on the history of economic thought. Economic Thought Before Adam Smith* (Vol. 1) Edward Elgar.
Rothbard, M. N. (1995). *An Austrian perspective on the history of economic thought. Classical Economics* (Vol. 2) Edward Elgar.
Rothbard, M. N. (2007). *The Betrayal of the American right.* Ludwig Von Mises Institute.
Rothbard, M. N. (2010). *Left and right: The prospects for liberty.* Ludwig von Moses Institute, Original work published 1965.
Rothbard, M. N. (2017). *The progressive Era* (P. Newman, ed.). Ludwig von Mises Institute.
Rothbard, M. N. (Forthcoming). The concepts 'rational' and 'irrational,' March 1954. In R. A. Modugno (Ed.), *Murray Rothbard on politics, philosophy, and history: A selection from his papers.* Ludwig von Mises Institute.
Rothbard, M. N. (Forthcoming). Memorandum on *catholicism, protestantism, and capitalism,* 1957a. In R. A. Modugno (Ed.), *Murray Rothbard on politics, philosophy, and history: a selection from his papers.* Ludwig von Mises Institute.
Rothbard, M. N. (Forthcoming). On Gustave de Molinari. December 1958. In R. A. Modugno (Ed.) *Murray Rothbard on politics, philosophy, and history: A selection from his papers.* Ludwig von Mises Institute.
Talmon, J. L. (1952). *The origins of totalitarian democracy.* Secker & Warburg.
Tierney, B. (1997). *The idea of natural rights: Studies on natural rights, natural law, and church law 1150–1625.* Scholars Press.
Urbinati, N. (2019). *Me the people: How populism transforms democracy.* Harvard University Press.
Weber, M. (2002). *The protestant ethic and the spirit of capitalism.* Penguin Books, Original work published 1904–1905.

CHAPTER 4

Rothbard the Political Scientist and Political Philosopher

Keywords Vietnam war · Constitutionalism · Aggression · State · New right · Anarchocapitalism · Environment · Ethics · Rationalism · Natural law

1 The Early 1970s: Militancy and the Political Project

In 1973, Rothbard published *For a New Liberty: The Libertarian Manifesto*. It is a text in which we find a deeply militant Rothbard who is very much affected by the historical, cultural, and political climate of those years. The most forceful theme in Rothbard's thought and militancy is his opposition to the United States involvement in the Vietnam War. These were years that brought to maturity Rothbard's detachment from the New Right and the formation of a conscious libertarian movement that was independent and opposed to any military and imperialist commitment of the United States in foreign policy. In the United States, peace movements had begun to mobilize, and a general discontent was spreading among the population. The October 1967 march of about fifty thousand citizens toward the Pentagon to express their discontent and opposition against the war is famous. During the Nixon presidency, the American anti-war protest escalated. People were calling for an end to the

R. A. Modugno, *The Legacy of Murray N. Rothbard*, Palgrave Studies in Austrian Economics,
https://doi.org/10.1007/978-3-032-06870-5_4

war, and, in fact, the war in Vietnam came to an end precisely because of the protests of American citizens who were no longer willing to bear its enormous costs—in terms of both economics and human lives. The Vietnam War, along with the Watergate scandal, only increased distrust toward the government, institutions, and power.

This immense distrust is expressed in *For a New Liberty*, where the state is described as "the supreme, the eternal, the best organized aggressor against the persons and property of the mass of the public .... If you wish to know how libertarians regard the State and any of its acts, simply think of the State as a criminal band" (Rothbard, 1973, pp. 56–57). From these premises begins a manifesto for a new political project—for a society without a state. The volume opens with a brief historical analysis of the doctrinal roots of libertarianism. Rothbard was very keen to search for the theoretical antecedents of libertarianism to emphasize its important tradition. He goes on to analyze the anatomy of the state and the reason for its criminal nature, address practical and concrete problems of society from a libertarian perspective, and outline the project of a stateless society. After the Second World War, the "social" qualification of the democratic state became the source of legitimization of political power in the West. The welfare state was widely embraced by the Great Society project of Presidents Kennedy and Johnson. Its ambition was to build a form of democracy capable of realizing ideals of social justice while guaranteeing both social rights and economic growth. The economic premises on which the welfare state was first based were formulated by John Maynard Keynes (1883–1946), and they continue to mark the economic policies of states to this day. With the publication of *The End of Laissez-Faire*, Keynes affirmed that capitalism had to be wisely governed and domesticated—otherwise, it would produce inequalities and social injustices (Keynes, 1927). With *The General Theory of Employment, Interest and Money*, he had paved the way for state intervention in order to stimulate consumption, achieve full employment, and ensure the stability of capitalism. This led to the mixed economy, where there is a high level of government intervention in the market (Keynes, 1936). Keynes subsequently provided a political-philosophical basis that went even further in strengthening the idea of a state redistributing wealth and able to achieve a just society, because this was a fair arrangement, according to John Rawls in *A Theory of Justice* (Rawls, 1971). It is precisely the redistributive and, consequently, coercive logic of the state that Rothbard condemns without appeal.

From the theoretical and historical point of view, for Rothbard, everything starts from the English Civil War of the seventeenth century and above all from the Levellers, who were the first, in his opinion, libertarians in history, elaborated the concept of self-ownership, fought against the absolute power of the sovereign, theorized the idea of a government limited in powers and functions, and became champions of freedom of trade and supporters of the sacredness of the right to private property. John Locke systematically rationalized that great ferment of ideas that characterized the period of the English Civil War, becoming the founding father of modern classical liberalism and firmly fixing the classic triad of natural rights: life, property, and freedom. Government is established on the basis of the consent of individuals for the purpose of safeguarding and protecting the natural and inalienable rights of human beings. These rights are inalienable because they cannot be separated from the very essence of the individual. This kind of government is the typical one conceived by classical liberalism—that is, one limited in powers and functions. Rothbard, however, lived through the reality of the failure of limited government, of a minimal state that—designed to protect the natural rights of individual life, liberty, property—has become the worst aggressor and has turned from a minimal state into a maximal state. In Rothbard's view, the real utopia is not a free society that protects and governs itself but a self-limiting state. But no matter how many constitutional limits a state places on political power, it will always tend to break the banks and go beyond those limits (Rothbard, 1973, pp. 420–426).

The great lesson of Montesquieu in *The Spirit of Laws* (Montesquieu, 1977) and Bolinbroke concerns the constitutionalist tradition—the tradition of checks and balances, a government limited by laws, a government of laws and not of men: citizens can control the government through free elections and through the sophisticated framework of constitutionalism that guarantees the rule of law. Moreover, nineteenth-century German legal doctrine theorized the idea of the Rechtsstaat—the rule of law—which limits itself to ensure the protection and respect of human rights and freedoms. The concept of the rule of law presupposes that the action of the state is always bound by and in accordance with the laws in force; therefore, the state subjects itself to respect for the rule of law, and this is done by means of a constitution. Georg Jellinek paid particular attention to the problem of the relationship between state power and the sphere of autonomy reserved for the individual. He worked toward the establishment of the Constitutional Court, advocating the idea of the state's self-restraint so that the people would be more willing to obey it.

Rothbard subjects to corrosive criticism the idea that the state can limit itself or that it has an interest in limiting itself. In fact, the whole idea of constitutionalism and a self-limiting rule of law clashes with the simple reality of the state's monopoly on violence, which admits no competitors. According to an effective and brilliant description by Anthony de Jasay, the state wears "a chastity belt," (de Jasay, 1985, p. 210), but if the key to the chastity belt is in the hands of the state, it will be very easy for it to open that belt and violate the freedom and property of its citizens. All the institutions that are supposed to control the state—the guardians of the constitution—are part of the state apparatus, and so it will be difficult for them to oppose the strategies of the state aimed at maximizing its discretionary power to dispose at will the fruits of taxation. The various constitutional courts and supreme courts are integral organs of the state apparatus, and the state is their employer—moreover, it is a monopolist. The theories of a government limited by law, such as that of Hayek's rule of law, are for Rothbard, a chimera—a utopia. As Marco Bassani notes, "Any written limitation that would leave the government free to interpret the extent of its own powers is doomed to fail and create an absolute and de facto unlimited power" (Bassani, 2011, p. lix). The rule of law has not been in a position to harness itself. In fact, how could one even think of handing over all the weapons and means of coercion to the monopoly state and saying to it, "Well, now limit yourself!" This seems like a utopian fantasy and the shortest way to an unlimited expansion of public powers.

Hayek himself, protagonist of the revival of constitutionalism, in the introduction to the latest edition of *Law, Legislation and Liberty*, recognizes, not without a certain bitterness, that

> when Montesquieu and the framers of the American Constitution articulated the conception of a limiting constitution that had grown up in England, they set a pattern which liberal constitutionalism has followed ever since. Their chief aim was to provide institutional safeguards of individual freedom; and the device in which they placed their faith was the separation of powers. In the form in which we know this division of power between the legislature, the judiciary and the administration, it has not achieved what it was meant to achieve. Governments everywhere have obtained by constitutional means powers which those men had meant to deny them. The first attempt to secure individual liberty by constitutions has evidently failed (Hayek, 2021, p. 63).

What is Rothbard's starting point for demonstrating the aggressive and criminal nature of the state? As we have seen, Rothbard has an axiomatic deductive approach, derived from Mises. The libertarian theory is based on an axiom that is the cornerstone of the Rothbardian system: the nonaggression axiom—that is, "that no man or group of men may aggress against the person or property of anyone else … . 'Aggression' is defined as the initiation of the use or threat of physical violence against the person or property of anyone else" (Rothbard, 1973, p. 27). Obviously, if every individual has the right to his property and must not be plundered by anyone—not even by the state—he also has the right to freely exchange his goods and donate or bequeath them to whomever he wishes without any kind of interference. This is why the libertarian is in favor of private property and a system of free markets—of laissez-faire. Rothbard summarizes the libertarian creed:

> While opposing any and all private or group aggression against the rights of person and property, the libertarian sees that throughout history and into the present day, there has been one central, dominant, and overriding aggressor upon all of these rights: the State. In contrast to all other thinkers, left, right, or in-between, the libertarian refuses to give the State the moral sanction to commit actions that almost everyone agrees would be immoral, illegal, and criminal if committed by any person or group in society. The libertarian, in short, insists on applying the general moral law to everyone, and makes no special exemptions for any person or group. But if we look at the State naked, as it were, we see that it is universally allowed, and even encouraged, to commit all the acts which even non-libertarians concede are reprehensible crimes. The State habitually commits mass murder, which it calls "war," or sometimes "suppression of subversion"; the State engages in enslavement into its military forces, which it calls "conscription"; and it lives and has its being in the practice of forcible theft, which it calls "taxation." The libertarian insists that whether or not such practices are supported by the majority of the population is not germane to their nature: that, regardless of popular sanction, War is Mass Murder, Conscription is Slavery, and Taxation is Robbery. The libertarian, in short, is almost completely the child in the fable, pointing out insistently that the emperor has no clothes (Rothbard, 1973, pp. 28–29).

While classical liberalism believes in the possibility of limiting the functions and powers of the state, considered as a necessary evil to ensure peaceful human coexistence, Rothbard revises and goes beyond this conception, considering the state as an evil and nothing more. The libertarian insists on applying the same ethical standard to both the individual and the state, but he is faced with a tradition of common feeling and politics going back five hundred years—that is, since the birth of the modern state. This historical tradition is the *raison d'état* that gained prominence exactly at the beginning of the modern age and went hand in hand with the emergence of the modern state. In 1589, Giovanni Botero published the treatise *The Reason of State*, in which he argued that, for the preservation of power and the salvation of the state, the state and all those acting in its name could carry out actions that would be considered crimes if committed by any private citizen (Botero, 2017). The other author inextricably linked to this theory is Niccolò Machiavelli, who in his classic work *The Prince* completely separates politics and morals. He thus introduces a double standard for ethical judgment—one for the actions of the state and its officials, and another for individuals who are subject to the rules dictated by the state itself (Machiavelli, 1961).

Why should no individual suffer aggressive depredation? What are the bases of the axiom of nonaggression? Rothbard recovers the typically Lockean natural law tradition that is the central theme of his 1980 work *The Ethics of Liberty*. Following Locke's discourse, Rothbard starts from an inalienable, natural, and self-evident right: self-ownership, the right that every individual holds to the ownership of himself and his body. From this right, following Locke's teaching, derives the right of private property, which is based on homesteading or the union of man's work—which belongs only to him—to natural resources. Private property is a right that represents an extension of the human personality, which combines something of itself with natural resources; therefore, the only legitimate titles of private property are those that derive from free exchange, voluntary donations, and inheritances. These considerations have significant implications for libertarian doctrine, particularly in pushing to their logical extremes and overcoming the typical implications of classical liberalism—of a state limited in powers and functions. "Freedom is a condition in which a person's ownership rights in his own body and his legitimate material property are *not* invaded, are not aggressed against," not even by the state (Rothbard, 1973, p. 50). For Rothbard, all human rights derive from the right to property. He criticizes the dichotomy typical of liberal thought that separates the right to private property from fundamental human rights. "Yet the two, according to the libertarian, are inextricably intertwined; they stand or fall together" (Rothbard, 1973, p. 51). What would become of freedom of speech or of the press if the state denied private property and owned or even controlled all printing presses, publishing houses, paper mills, and assembly halls? Let us return to the vision of the state as an aggressor. "Libertarians regard the State as the supreme, the eternal, the best organized aggressor against the persons and property of the mass of the public … . If you wish to know how libertarians regard the State and any of its acts, simply think of the State as a criminal band" (Rothbard, 1973, pp. 56–57). Rothbard echoes the distinctions made earlier by Franz Oppenheimer and Albert Jay Nock, according to which people in society derive their resources from production, exchange, free gifts, and inheritances, while the government procures its income through violence and coercion—that is, taxation and the threat of sanctions and imprisonment if payment does not arrive. Only the government has the power to attack the property of citizens, although it claims that taxation benefits the public interest and common good. But it is impossible for the state to know the good and interests of every individual. Consequently, the government itself decides and chooses what goods and values to achieve, depriving people of the freedom to choose what is best for them, what values to achieve, and what to do with their lives. The state, through taxation and redistribution of resources, imposes its own moral code, which obviously does not suit everyone, because every human being is unique. If the goal of the libertarian is not merely to minimize coercion within society, as the classical liberal aims to do, but to eliminate it entirely, then the logical conclusion is that the state should be abolished.

It is often said that we are the state. But is this true? Rothbard is fully aware of the theory of elites when he writes, "If the State is a group of plunderers, *who* then constitutes the State? Clearly, the ruling elite consists at any time of (a) the full-time *apparatus*—the kings, politicians, and bureaucrats who man and operate the State; and (b) the groups who have maneuvered to gain privileges, subsidies, and benefices from the State. The remainder of society constitutes the ruled … . The very nature of government creates two unequal and inherently conflicting classes in society: those who, on net, *pay* the taxes (the 'tax-payers'), and those who, on net, *live off* taxes (the 'tax-consumers')" (Rothbard, 1973, p. 64). But how is it that every government, despite the considerable level of coercion exerted on the population, obtains the consent of the governed? How does the government stand on consensus? As Étienne de La Boétie brilliantly guessed in the sixteenth century, when he was just a boy,

> a single tyrant who has no other power than the power they give him ... he has indeed nothing more than the power that you confer upon him to destroy you .... How does he have any power over you except through you? Resolve to serve no more, and you are at once freed. I do not ask that you place hands upon the tyrant to topple him over, but simply that you support him no longer; then you will behold him, like a great Colossus whose pedestal has been pulled away, fall of his own weight and break into pieces (La Boétie, 1975, pp. 42, 48–49).

Why does the only answer to the problem of civil coexistence—of the political order—seem to be the state? The answer would seem simple: as Thomas Hobbes wrote, the life of man outside the state is "solitary, poore, nasty, brutish, and short" (Hobbes, 2012, p. 192). But is it really so? This is where intellectuals and their role in building consensus for the state in exchange for prestigious and lucrative positions come into play.

Initially, it was the clergy—the sovereign's first advisers—who convinced the population that he reigned by a divine right transmitted directly to him by God and that the people owed obedience to this benevolent father of the nation. Just as one owed obedience to the pater familias that reflected the divine power within the family—as explained by Jean Bodin, the greatest theorist of modern sovereignty—so too obedience was due to the sovereign. The universe had a single sun, the kingdom of France a single king, and the family a single head in the pater familias (Bodin, 1992). Later, it was the jurists who supported the state, and today a fundamental role is played by economists. In general, there is an interdisciplinary plethora of intellectuals ready to support and spread the goodness of the statist message. The state obtains consent by claiming that taxation serves the common good and social justice. Meanwhile, intellectuals defend the state's theory of justice and equity to the very people being plundered by it. The state is composed of particularly wise men able to correct distortions in the market as well as the egoism involved in free bargaining between individuals. The so-called *chair socialists* are a clear example of an alliance between the state and intellectuals. These nineteenth-century professors at the University of Berlin would "form themselves into what they themselves proclaimed as the bodyguard of the House of Hohenzollern" (Rothbard, 1973, pp. 74–75). In more recent times, economists have explained the miracles of the Keynesian multiplier—government spending that stimulates consumption and gets the economy moving again. Then there is the great theme of public goods—that is, all those goods that the market would have no interest in producing due to the lack of economic incentive, often because of free riders who would use the good without paying the cost. These include large infrastructure such as bridges, highways, roads, and public parks. Then there are sectors that have long been regarded as natural monopolies. Because their monopolistic nature is contrary to the public interest, it is good that the state should take charge of them, since it is the only entity capable of achieving the common good and selling certain goods and services at a fair price—although not determined by the market but by an enlightened centralized planner. Goods and services that have long been considered state monopolies include railways, post offices, telephony, and electricity.

2 Problems and Practical Proposals for a Libertarian Society

At this point, Rothbard gets to the heart of his political proposal. He does so by starting with one of the most topical issues at that time: compulsory conscription. In 1969, it seemed like the right time to give a more formal organization to the libertarian movement with the Radical Libertarian Alliance. This Rothbardian association decided to join the only youth organization of the American right, Young Americans for Freedom, on the common ground of challenging Buckley on the two focal points of the Vietnam War and conscription. A famous convention was held in St. Louis on August 15, 1969, in which a draft card was burned.

People are convinced that slavery no longer exists in the United States, but what is conscription if not slavery? Involuntary servitude? The moment a young man receives his draft card, "his body and will are no longer his own; he is subject to the dictates of the government; and he can be forced to kill and to place his own life in jeopardy if the authorities so decree. What else is involuntary servitude if not the draft?" (Rothbard, 1973, p. 98) This is an inadmissible act of assault, kidnapping, and possibly murder. In the name of what is all this justified? In the name of the homeland and of society. But the homeland and society consist of all citizens—excepting, it would seem, the young conscripts, who are just abstractions used to mask the interests of specific individuals. Not only that, but desertion carries severe penalties, from incarceration to capital punishment. From here, Rothbard goes on to reproach the American government for having forgotten a principle dear to Thomas Jefferson: opposition to the establishment of a standing army. A state with a standing army will always be tempted to use it to attack or implement an imperialist policy. In the event of aggression, Jefferson believed in the civic militia, composed of volunteer citizens ready to defend their country.

Next, Rothbard tackles the broad issue of civil rights from a libertarian perspective, starting with freedom of speech. "Freedom of speech will necessarily be upheld to the uttermost by every libertarian. Freedom to say, print, and sell any utterance becomes an absolute right, in whatever area the speech or expression chooses to cover" (Rothbard, 1973, p. 115). There are certainly borderline cases that can be very controversial—for example, inciting a riot, in which case the act can be considered immoral, but, if it does not result in a criminal act and no riot occurs, it should be seen as defending a cause rather than a crime. Another controversial issue is defamation or slander. A person's reputation is certainly important, but people may have different subjective feelings about a particular person. Defamation does not invade either the person or the property of an individual; therefore, it should not be considered punishable by law. Obviously, defamation is an immoral act, but the libertarian always emphasizes the difference between morality and legality. Rothbard then adds an observation that was evidently valid in the years in which he wrote but that today concerns us very closely: "Fortunately, in recent years the laws against libel have been progressively weakened, so that one can now deliver vigorous and trenchant criticisms of public officials and of people in the public eye without fear of being subject to costly legal action or legal punishment" (Rothbard, 1973, p. 117). One wonders what Rothbard would think of our Western society, in which the concept of political correctness has expanded to the point of exasperation—and to the point that there are laws against hatred. The simple social norms of "good manners" are no longer sufficient for self-control and interpersonal relationships. Many are calling for government intervention to force people to behave in a civilized manner. We are in the midst of a nightmarish moment in which freedom of thought is restricted and freedom as a political ideal is in decline. This is the consequence, on the one hand, of a long process of domesticating intellectuals and, on the other, of the inexorable march of power and the state in the lives of citizens.

Directly related to the issue of freedom of speech are media such as radio and television. Rothbard recalls that in 1927, the federal government nationalized the airwaves with the Radio Act, then granted private stations licenses to use the frequencies. The successive multiplication of radio and television stations has meant that government control over stations has weakened significantly. Pay-TV, in particular, focuses on its own audiences and develops specialized markets for certain kinds of viewers. The libertarian attitude is, of course, to treat the media as we treat books and newspapers—by rejecting any form of government interference in its expression.

Other highly controversial and thorny issues include pornography, prostitution, and abortion. Conservatives, Rothbard notes, say pornography is degrading and immoral and should be banned. The central problem is that the morality of pornography—whether its consequences are good or bad—has nothing to do with its legality. It is not the job of the state to make individuals moral or upright. Everyone must be free to adopt moral behavior or not; otherwise, by depriving man of free will, a right and moral choice is deprived of authentic value. In addition, Rothbard introduces the important concept of *no victims, no crimes.* Behavior may be morally reprehensible, but if it does not involve the violation of the person and property of others, it is not a crime and cannot be banned by law. Of course, this does not mean that Rothbard or, in general, a libertarian should approve of immoral actions. Currently, the pornography industry involves only consenting adults and no aggression; therefore, it does not involve any crime and cannot be banned. To prohibit it would, among other things, infringe on the right of others to produce, sell, buy, and possess pornographic material.

> The liberal would ban films of violence, unesthetic advertising, football, and racial discrimination, and, at the extreme, place everyone in a "Skinner box" to be run by a supposedly benevolent liberal dictator. But the effect would be the same: to reduce everyone to a subhuman level and to deprive everyone of the most precious part of his or her humanity—the freedom to choose. The irony, of course, is that by forcing men to be "moral"— i.e., to *act* morally—the conservative or liberal jailkeepers would in reality deprive men of the very *possibility* of being moral. The concept of "morality" makes no sense unless the moral act is freely chosen (Rothbard, 1973, p. 128).

The argument is quite similar for prostitution. Any relationship between consenting adults, including the purchase and sale of sexual services, is considered legal by the libertarian—provided, of course, that there are no forms of aggression against the person or property. Again, this is not to say that Rothbard or libertarians approve of certain acts. But while those acts may be considered morally reprehensible, that does not make them crimes. *No victims, no crimes* is the motto of the libertarian regarding such topics. Moreover, prohibiting brothels means transferring prostitution to the streets, where it will generate even more crime. When the state prohibits such activities, it creates a black market. Every individual is the owner of himself, and a woman who owns her person and body must also be perfectly free to sell sexual services. Rothbard's approach to prostitution is identical to that of Wendy McElroy; the theoretical maxim of libertarian feminism, or, as she calls it, *ifeminism*. McElroy acknowledges her intellectual debt to Rothbard for making her an anarchocapitalist. It should also be noted that prostitution is illegal in the United States but regulated only in Nevada (On this see McElroy, 1991). With regard to what he generically calls sexual legislation, Rothbard points out that sex intimately concerns the personal sphere, and it is therefore inadmissible for the government to interfere with it—with the exception of rape: "Violent acts such as rape, of course, are to be classed as crimes in the same way as any other act of violence against persons" (Rothbard, 1973, p. 129). Rothbard criticizes cases in which rapists, though found guilty, are treated less severely than other criminals, while the victim is blamed—often for allegedly being provocative. "Clearly, an impermissible sexual double standard has been at work" (Rothbard, 1973, pp. 129–130).

Rothbard's defense of abortion is also exclusively grounded in the right of self-ownership. He does not underestimate the moral or even Catholic arguments against abortion, but the central issue is whether abortion can be considered murder. From here ensues a series of endless disquisitions, Rothbard notes, by doctors, scientists, and theologians to try to understand when life actually begins—whether at conception or later, and if later, when. But while all this is certainly very relevant from the point of view of the morality of abortion, it is not at all relevant, for a libertarian, from the point of view of the legality of abortion. The Rothbardian position is very clear:

> But there is more involved here, and this is the crucial consideration. If we are to treat the fetus as having the same rights as humans, then let us ask:

> What *human* has the right to remain, unbidden, as an unwanted parasite within some other human being's body? This is the nub of the issue: the absolute right of every person and hence every woman, to the ownership of her own body. What the mother is doing in an abortion is causing an unwanted entity within her body to be ejected from it: If the fetus dies, this does not rebut the point that no being has a right to live, unbidden, as a parasite within or upon some person's body (Rothbard, 1973, p. 132).

Only the woman has the right to accept her pregnancy or not. Libertarian feminist and Rothbardian Wendy McElroy's position on the issue is slightly different. McElroy describes herself as pro-choice, defending the practice on the basis of a woman's right to self-ownership—so far, this is strictly Rothbardian. She adds, however, that the fetus becomes an individual endowed with rights of self-ownership, life, freedom, and property only when it detaches itself from the mother's body and not before. The Rothbardian "unwanted parasite" is, therefore, a human being but not yet endowed with individual rights (McElroy, 1991).

Other prohibitions examined by Rothbard include those against gambling, drugs, police corruption, and the right to bear arms. Rothbard is totally opposed to a paternalistic conception of the state—a state that watches over its citizens, their morality, and their physical well-being, including their intake of harmful substances. Being free means rejecting the notion that government should protect us from ourselves; therefore, laws that prohibit gambling are absurd to Rothbard. Everyone should be free to do what he sees fit with his possessions, even at the risk of losing them. It is not the state's job to prevent an individual from risking his savings or to ensure that his behavior is moral. The same applies to drug use and the war on drugs. Drugs are bad for your health, addictive, and often lead to theft to obtain doses at exorbitant prices, but here we enter the realm of the failures of prohibitionist policies. If drugs were legal, their availability would be greater, prices would be affordable, and the black market, with its corollaries of theft and crime, would disappear. How much prohibitionist policies have failed has already been demonstrated by the 1920s prohibition of alcohol. A thriving black market developed, while crime and even alcohol consumption increased (Thornton, 1991). Certainly, taking drugs is bad, as is abusing alcohol, but so is eating too much fat, getting too much sun, and smoking tobacco. Just as the state does not make it illegal to sunbathe or eat too much fat, so too should it leave people free to be responsible for themselves and their health—and therefore also to harm themselves and pay for their actions. As John Stuart Mill argued, the state is justified in intervening in the private sphere of one individual only to protect other individuals from aggression (Mill, 1991). As for corruption among the police, Rothbard notes that often when a police officer is bribed, he turns a blind eye to things that the state has decided are crimes—drug use, prostitution, and gambling—but if the state did not consider such actions illegal, there would be no opportunity for corruption in the first place. It is impossible not to trace these Rothbardian considerations back to a text that caused a sensation and has become a classic of libertarian literature: Walter Block's *Defending the Undefendable* (Block, 2018).

Another issue very dear to Rothbard and libertarians, but very controversial, is that of the right to bear arms. One of the principles that paved the way for the modern state was the disarmament of the population so that the state's offer of monopoly protection could not be refused (Brunner, 1939). The idea was that only the state and its armed forces could possess weapons. But the Second Amendment to the US Constitution established the opposing principle that "the right of the people to keep and bear arms, shall not be infringed." Rothbard is convinced that every individual has the right to use a weapon to protect himself from the aggression of criminals, but there has developed in the United States a certain tendency to partially erode this right. The state of New York, as well as other states, has introduced limitations on the right to freely acquire weapons, thus providing a clear advantage to criminals and preventing individual citizens from intervening in defense of others when needed—undermining solidarity among citizens. The right to bear arms is an issue that continues to worry libertarians to this day; for example, Andrew Napolitano, a former justice of the New Jersey Supreme Court, has expressed concern over the debate about whether it is lawful for private citizens to carry firearms—especially when that right is questioned due to the misuse of a weapon by someone else. He cites the important *District of Columbia v. Heller* (2008), which states that the right to bear arms must be considered a pre-political individual right—that is, a fundamental right. This right is considered the highest level of protection conceived by American law. If the government has the right to be armed, the citizens must have the same right, and it would be absurd to say that it is constitutional to deprive citizens of a fundamental right because of the bad behavior of others. Instead, those who break the law must be prosecuted more vigorously (Napolitano, 2019, pp. 4–5).

An unassailable symbol of democratic states is the public and compulsory education system. Children up to a certain age, which has increased over time, are obligated to attend public or private schools whose curricula, in either case, have been authorized and certified by the state. The almost sacred view of compulsory school attendance is based on the assumption—also untouchable—that all individuals, whatever social class they belong to, must have the same opportunity to access education. But the question, in Rothbard's view, is misplaced. The issue owes a great intellectual debt to the Old Right, which has been cited abundantly on this subject. First of all, just as Nock, Mencken, and Paterson thought, all human beings are different from each other, and not all are equally educable or inclined to study the same things. Forcing millions of recalcitrant children and young people to attend educational institutions to qualify for a job very often means churning out the unhappy and frustrated. Rothbard, like Nock and Mencken, rejects mass schooling as based on the egalitarian belief of the educability of every child. All this means not only distorting the lives of those who would prefer to work early rather than go to school, but also lowering the quality of education due to the necessity of putting it within everyone's reach. This leads to poor educational outcomes and the destruction of excellence.

Moreover, if the masses are to be educated in public or government-authorized schools, these will become a powerful means of regimentation, designed to inculcate in the minds of citizens whatever civic virtues the state desires as well as obedience to public authority. For Rothbard, the main reason the state pushed for public schools and compulsory schooling was to obtain a uniform and obedient population. The more education becomes public, the more it translates into the destruction of individuality. But if education were exclusively private and free from any government interference, then parents could be free to choose the most suitable schools for their children. This would involve a free market of schools (Rothbard, 1973, pp. 145–154). Rothbard echoes Paterson's words: "Every politically controlled educational system will inculcate the doctrine on state supremacy sooner or later … . Once that doctrine has been accepted, it becomes an almost superhuman task to break the stranglehold of the political power over the life of the citizen. It has had his body, property, and mind in its clutches from infancy … . A tax supported, compulsory educational system is the complete model of the totalitarian state" (Paterson, 1996, p. 258).

The school voucher proposed by Milton Friedman would improve parental freedom of choice but would not solve the issue of financing education through the coercive taxation of single people and childless couples. Rothbard particularly admires the homeschooling model, where parents, especially for primary education, can educate their own children, doing this work from home. Homeschooling is an educational system that has not been spared criticism, especially for its lack of socialization, but many parents arrange for their children to socialize in places besides school.

But what about the welfare state? If, on the one hand, the *social* connotation of the state, with its guarantee of social rights, has seemed to become, since the Second World War, the source of legitimacy for the very existence of the state, it is undeniable, on the other hand, that during the 1970s the welfare state entered into crisis, in part because of the oil crisis of 1973 that forced Western democracies to deal with reality, but also due to the simple fact that economic growth has its limitations. For Rothbard, the welfare state is a large system in which "every person on the welfare dole used to feel, the stigma of being parasitic and living off production instead of contributing to production" (Rothbard, 1973, p. 180). Yet living standards have been improving since the 1930s, so the increase in welfare and its beneficiaries cannot be traced back to poverty. The real problem, for Rothbard, is that largely as a result of the spread of liberal ideology, incentives to live on public assistance have increased rather than decreased. If welfare is increasingly presented as a right and taxation increases as financing social assistance, then it will be more convenient to live on public charity than to go to work and be taxed! Moreover, Rothbard points out, depending on government support was seen—even by the beneficiary himself—as something to be ashamed of. In the past, the typical role of the social worker was to help the needy to help themselves—that is, to find a job and see themselves once again as individuals endowed with dignity and able to stand on their own two feet. But now the typical liberal social worker convinces those in difficult circumstances to see themselves as entitled to benefits, thereby contributing to the growing number of people who prefer to live on public assistance.

At one time, before the state became *social* after the Second World War and assumed the role of wealth redistributor, the concept of social assistance was decidedly libertarian. It was based on the idea that all subsidies should come exclusively from private initiatives, charities, and voluntary institutions. Consider the important role played by the English aristocracy in caring for the needy: the nobility ran schools, hospitals, and charities. The same is true for the church, which for centuries has managed charities and other important services. The libertarian position calls for the complete abolition of government assistance, preferring private charity and a broader role for civil society. Authentic charity requires sincere solidarity, friendship, and the desire to restore self-respect and self-reliance to the individual. Moreover, as some historical studies have highlighted, institutions such as the mutual aid societies in America and England during the nineteenth century provided their members with medical care, unemployment insurance, social security, health insurance, and other services that are now the prerogative of the welfare state. These were not institutions whose role was marginal—in fact, when the British government's National Insurance Act of 1911 established compulsory social security for twelve million people, voluntary insurance—especially mutual aid societies—already covered at least nine million people (Green, 2002, p. 205; Beito, 2002, pp. 182–203).

The liberal attitude of the left, on the other hand, promotes the idea of public welfare as a just moral claim and a right, dissuades the poor from looking for jobs, encourages the lack of desire to work and rely on themselves, and deprives the poor of the assistance of civil society and the church. In short, the government should simply get out of the way—by reducing the tax burden, freeing the productive forces of civil society, and eliminating laws, permits, licenses, and the thousands of bureaucratic snares that hinder anyone trying to start a small business. Rothbard cites the humble itinerant trades that allowed many immigrants to support themselves and eventually grow into successful entrepreneurs and business owners. Finally, the government should eliminate the minimum wage laws, which, as noted above, do nothing but create unemployment, excluding from the labor market workers who would be willing to work even for a low wage.

2.1 Against Keynes

The 1973 oil crisis marked the end of postwar economic growth. The economic uncertainty of the two-year period 1973–74 framed the crisis of the fiscal apparatus and the economic role of the state, which was increasingly seen as a producer not of wealth but of public debt. Until the early 1970s, the Keynesians had been the undisputed rulers of the economic scene; however, not only had Keynesian policies not eliminated inflation but, in those years, increased it dramatically. At the same time, the United States experienced a deep economic crisis. All this brought classical liberalism and Mises's analysis back to the fore, since the occurrence of these phenomena meant that there must be something deeply wrong with the Keynesian recipe.

> Economists had always known that either the economy is in a boom period, in which case prices are rising, *or else* the economy is in a recession or depression marked by high unemployment, in which case prices are falling. In the boom, the Keynesian government was supposed to "sop up excess purchasing power" by increasing taxes, according to the Keynesian prescription—that is, it was supposed to take spending out of the economy; in the recession, on the other hand, the government was supposed to increase its spending and its deficits, in order to pump spending into the economy. But if the economy should be in an inflation *and* a recession with heavy unemployment *at the same time*, what in the world was government supposed to do? How could it step on the economic accelerator *and* brake at the same time? (Rothbard, 1973, p. 214)

Such an inflationary recession, or stagflation, which characterized the American economy in 1973–1974, enabled Rothbard to highlight the crucial weakness of Keynesian economics and its explanation of the Great Depression, which, since the 1936 publication of Keynes's *General Theory of Employment, Interest and Money*, had dominated the economic scene as the mainstream theory. According to Keynes, economic depressions result from insufficient spending, while inflation is due to overspending. In a period of depression, the government's job is to increase the amount of money spent. Inflation—that is, a generalized rise in prices—indicates that the government must act in a way that reduces spending. Stagflation is the presence of an economic depression and a generalized increase in prices at the same time, which Keynesian theory had thought to be impossible.

If Keynes's theory is wrong, Rothbard argues, then the real explanation lies in the Misesian theory of the business cycle—also known as the Austrian theory. This theory attributes depression to an expansion of bank credit, corresponding to the artificial lowering of the interest rate of money. An artificially low interest rate entices businessmen to increase investment spending. Such an increase in investment, however, does not occur in accordance with the time preferences of consumers—that is, their preferences for goods in the present rather than the future. But it is precisely the time preferences of consumers that determine the natural interest rate, which means that when the expansion of bank credit stops, the interest rate of money will rise again, at which point investments that were made following the lowering of the interest rate will have to be liquidated. This liquidation process is the economic depression and is necessary for the economy to return to solid foundations.

The government should not do anything to interfere with this process, which is necessary to return to a healthy economy. Not only Mises and Rothbard but also Friedrich von Hayek, a pupil of Mises, remained firmly anchored to this theory.

2.2 Public Works, Security, and Justice

We now move on to the pars construens: the Rothbardian society that functions without a state apparatus—deprived, to use Max Weber's famous definition, of the monopoly of the use of force and the administration of justice for a given territory. The state does not tolerate competitors in the exercise of these two functions, but Rothbard tries to imagine a plurality of police and judicial agencies for the same territory and in competition with each other.

First of all, all roads, bridges, and highways would be the property of individuals, groups, businesses, or cooperatives of individuals—merchants in some areas, homeowners in others. Police services would be offered to protect customers. Homeowners would have an interest in their neighborhoods being safe, and they would carry out timely maintenance of their roads to avoid lowering the value of their properties. The problem of police brutality in America, Rothbard notes, would disappear with private police companies paid directly by traders or landlords. Roads, highways, and bridges would be paid for with tolls. Rothbard recalls how the first truly efficient and safe road networks in the United States were funded by private companies, citizens' associations, landowners, and private railroads.

But who will manage the administration of justice and the protection of citizens without the state monopoly? Rothbard admits that this is the hardest thing to imagine. The assumption is that all services should be marketable—that is, offered by the market under free competition—including protection against aggression and administration of justice. There are many private police companies operating inside shopping malls, for example. Moreover, state services are by no means free but are financed by taxes. Under a system of free competition, people could voluntarily insure themselves by paying companies that offer integrated private police and administration of justice services. Judges could offer privatized legal expertise and authority, in exchange for remuneration, to settle disputes and administer justice.

Before the birth of the modern state, between the end of the fifteenth century and the sixteenth century, there was no body of judges directly reporting to the sovereign. Judges were legal scholars and experts called to settle disputes and administer justice—they were private professionals. Anyone who needed it tried to get the advice of the best professional. In the contemporary world, the poor, Rothbard points out, would be helped by private charities, which would flourish thanks to a new empowerment of civil society. In *For a New Liberty*, Rothbard expands the discourse on protection agencies already introduced a few years earlier in *Power and Market* and "On Gustave de Molinari." He makes the case for free market anarchism, as underlined by Walter Block (2021, p. 7).

What libertarian code would apply in a society without the monopolistic production of law—without rights made and undone by a sovereign or parliament? Rothbard, citing "the libertarian Italian jurist Bruno Leoni," (Rothbard, 1973, p. 283), recalls the experience of the English common law courts, which did not operate on the basis of politically enacted laws but rather on customary law discovered by judges, grounded in precedent, and validated by the consent of generations over the centuries. Why is custom distinguished from the state and its monopolistic production of law? Perhaps the most comprehensive answer comes from Jean Bodin, the greatest theorist of sovereignty during the rise of the modern state in the sixteenth century:

> Private persons make the customs, which can be general as well as local. Custom, surely, has no less power than law, and as the prince is master of the law [it is objected], private persons are masters of the customs. I answer that custom acquires its force little by little and by the common consent of all, or most, over many years, while law appears suddenly, and gets its strength from one person who has the power of commanding all. Custom slips in softly and without violence; law is commanded and promulgated by power, very often against the subjects' wishes (Bodin, 1992, p. 57).

But to establish a truly libertarian legal code for the anarchocapitalist society envisioned by Rothbard, it is not enough to rely on precedent or tradition. Some aspects of the common law may not be compatible with libertarian principles, in which case the reference point must always be the principle of nonaggression toward the person and his property. It is this principle that makes it possible to amend the common law and obtain a genuinely libertarian legal code.

Can the principle of nonaggression also provide answers to the complex problems of environmental protection and pollution? One starting point might be to examine the blame directed at free market capitalism. Initially, the fear was that it would lead to increasing poverty. Later, critics complained of an excessive well-being that tended toward materialism and alienation from spiritual values. Subsequently, there were concerns that the development of new automated production technologies would lead to mass unemployment. Again, well-being becomes excessive and a source of pollution—a rapid rush to the exhaustion of resources. The proposed solution is for the state to intervene and put a stop to capitalism deemed to be growing too rapidly. Rothbard wrote all this in 1970. He also pointed out that the free market has become a convenient scapegoat to blame for everything negative that happens in the world (Rothbard, 2000, pp. 175–189). Not much has changed since those remarks. Rothbard complains, in fact, about the attack by the

> comfortable, contented upper-class liberals. Enjoying a material contentment and a living standard undreamt of by even the wealthiest men of the past, it is easy for upper-class liberals to sneer at "materialism," and to call for a freeze on all further economic advance. For the mass of the world's population still living in squalor such a cry for the cessation of growth is truly obscene … . The widespread attack on technology is even more irresponsible. If technology were to be rolled back to the "tribe" and to the preindustrial era, the result would be mass starvation and death on a universal scale (Rothbard, 1973, p. 305).

Today, a clear example of certain intellectual tendencies is well represented by Serge Latouche and his *Petit traité de la décroissance sereine* (Latouche, 2007). There is a need, however, then as now, for greater economic growth and increasingly sophisticated technologies that offer everyone higher standards of living and greater possibilities for devotion to cultural and spiritual interests.

Rothbard was very skeptical of the predictions of the Club of Rome, founded in 1968, about the exhaustion of natural resources such as oil within 40 years. The years have passed and natural resources have not been exhausted, yet we keep saying that there is no more time and that limits must be placed on development to avoid climate change and ecological disaster due to carbon dioxide emissions.[1] Actually, Rothbard points out,

[1] The Club of Rome, founded in 1968 and based in Switzerland, wanted to be a cenacle of thinkers dedicated to analyzing the changes in contemporary society and defining the limits of development. Its mission is to act as a catalyst for global change, identifying the main

neither statism nor socialism has proved effective in solving pollution problems. Water pollution, for example, can only be seriously addressed by the recognition and protection of private property rights over water. The owners of rivers and lakes would immediately sue anyone who violated their property rights—that is, the pollution of their own resources would demand compensation for damages. In the same way, the air pollution that harms the health of people, cultivated fields, and orchards could be stopped if the police and courts recognized and protected property rights (Rothbard, 2000, pp. 175–189). The remedy, therefore, is not less capitalism and more state but the incentive to develop fewer polluting technologies. Johan Norberg's 2016 book *Progress: Ten Reasons to Look Forward to the Future* discusses greenhouse gases and carbon dioxide emissions, using eloquent research and statistics to show that free market capitalism is not to blame for pollution. In short, technology and well-being are not at all an obstacle to environmental sustainability but a precondition. The most polluting places are not the most technologically advanced ones, such as New York, London, and Paris, but the most backward or developing ones, such as Beijing and New Delhi. The richer a country is, the more it will be incentivized to invest in and seek out technological solutions that are compatible with the environment, while the most serious environmental problems come from poor countries (Norberg, 2016).

But, Rothbard asks, what would happen to a libertarian society if it were attacked by an enemy—for example, Russia? First, in his opinion, history teaches us that wars arise essentially from conflicts between nation-states. Furthermore, "the main reason a conquering country can rule a defeated country is that the latter has an existing State apparatus to transmit and enforce the victor's orders onto a subject population" (Rothbard, 1973, p. 298). In an anarchocapitalist society, the Russian army would not find any state apparatus to conquer, but it would be faced with an armed population, which would be ready to defend its freedom through a guerrilla war and, according to Rothbard, would prove to be an irresistible force.

problems that humanity will face, analyzing them in a global context, and seeking alternative solutions in different possible scenarios. In recent years, Greta Thunberg has advocated the school strike for the climate change issue, and it continues to insist that environmental disasters will soon occur if no limits are placed on economic development.

If Rothbard's concrete project is his entirely new proposal for anarcho-capitalism, to whom is it addressed? And how can one hope to achieve it? He often wondered about what strategy libertarians should follow. Already in 1961, at the conference for the foundation of the Institute for Humane Studies, he focused on precisely this theme (Rothbard, 1961, forthcoming). In those years, libertarians were essentially economists, but Rothbard hoped for and emphasized the importance of founding a science of freedom that would be interdisciplinary. Rothbard's strategy is essentially cultural and aims to involve as many disciplines as possible—philosophy, political science, law, psychology, economics, history, and sociology. He anticipates a theme that will be central in the 1982 classic *The Ethics of Liberty*—namely, the revaluation of political philosophy such that the political scientist can make value judgments and natural law—rather than utilitarianism or consequentialism—becomes the basis for an ethics of freedom. *For a New Liberty* emphasizes the importance of education to the culture of freedom—an idea that seems to agree with the Gramscian strategic perspective—to convince the intellectual ruling classes of the value of an ethics based on absolute ownership of oneself, one's own limbs, and the results of one's work. But Rothbard also distrusts gradualism and reformist policies. He considers himself an abolitionist who wants to achieve his anti-statist goals as effectively and quickly as possible. But does such a way exist? Leonard E. Read said that if there were a button for the immediate abolition of the price and wage controls put in place after the Second World War, he would not hesitate to press it. But there is no button for abolishing the state, so cultural diffusion and conviction are fundamental. Rothbard, however, is not addressing the intellectual elites—he does not address groups or classes—but rather individuals, specifically those most harassed by the state and its bureaucratic apparatus—not the big businessman colluding with the state but rather the middle class individual, the small trader, the small entrepreneur, and young people in general. In doing so, he takes up a very suggestive passage by Hayek:

> We must make the building of a free society once more an intellectual adventure, a deed of courage. What we lack is a liberal Utopia, a program which seems neither a mere defense of things as they are nor a diluted kind of socialism, but a truly liberal radicalism which does not spare the susceptibilities of the mighty ... which is not too severely practical, and which does not confine itself to what appears today as politically possible .... Free trade and freedom of opportunity are ideals which still may arouse the

> imaginations of large numbers, but a mere "reasonable freedom of trade" or a mere "relaxation of controls" is neither intellectually respectable nor likely to inspire any enthusiasm .... But if we can regain that belief in the power of ideas which was the mark of liberalism at its best, the battle is not lost (Hayek, 1949, p. 384).

Rothbard's intellectual adventure certainly satisfies this need.

2.3 *Foreign Policy*

Rothbard approaches foreign policy pragmatically—that is, not in relation to a hypothetical anarchocapitalist world but to the existing world, a world of nation-states—examining its forms in America during the twentieth century. First, he claims that the term *isolationist* is misleading. The Old Right had been labeled as such since the 1930s for opposing American involvement in the World Wars, but their objection was specifically to interventionist and imperialist foreign policy—not to trade or broader international engagement. In reality, foreign policy anti-interventionists have never advocated policies of isolation. They were rather "men who opposed the aggrandizement of the nation-state and favored peace, free trade, free migration and peaceful cultural exchanges among peoples of all nations" (Rothbard, 1973, p. 330). War is mass murder and the worst crime that can be committed. With the birth of the modern state, the subsequent development of weapons of mass destruction, the emergence of standing armies under the centralized state, and the involvement and slaughter of innocent civilians became integral parts of warfare. Rothbard also polemicizes against the myth of collective security—namely, the idea that if one state is attacked, another state friendly to the victim must come to its rescue. Truman saw this as an act of policing, but it only widened the conflict and involved citizens of other states in the mass murder. The only case in which state violence is acceptable to a libertarian is defense against aggression. No state should interfere in the foreign policy of other states.

Rothbard succinctly defines the United States as the "most warlike, most interventionist, most imperialist government" (Rothbard, 1973, p. 369) of the twentieth century. Since President Wilson's foreign policy, America has assumed the role of the world's policeman and guarantor of democracy, as if it were the country endowed with a predestined role—a manifest destiny aimed at exporting its model of freedom and justice to the rest of the world. Rothbard cites the appropriation of the Philippines, the dominance over

Cuba, the Korean War, and, of course, the great American trauma of the Vietnam War. In short, the American state, considering itself the policeman of the world, "has itself become a great and continuing aggressor" (Rothbard, 1973, p. 330). On the contrary, Soviet foreign policy, in his view, is not an imperialist policy. Because, according to Marxism, the communist revolution is something inevitable—the natural unfolding of history—exporting communism would not make sense. Moreover, Rothbard notes that the foreign policy of the Soviet Union after the Second World War basically did nothing but try to preserve the borders of the Soviet bloc. Here, Rothbard seems to want to bend a historical reality of totalitarianism and violence to his own personal analysis, forgetting that, as Hannah Arendt explains, totalitarianism is always imperialist and one of its characteristics is its tendency to expand (Arendt, 1951).

In my opinion, this should not be confused with some sort of anti-Americanism on the part of Rothbard. First, war is one of the greatest opportunities for the state to increase its power of interference in and control over society. It is no coincidence that Rothbard recalls with Randolph Bourne that "war is essentially the health of the State" (Bourne, 1998, p. 9). Second, Rothbard recalls and regrets the libertarian roots of the founding of the American republic. He wants to recover the Jeffersonian values of the struggle for human freedom that are the heart and soul of his country. This detailed struggle between power and freedom is easy to see in Rothbard's five-volume American history from the colonies to the War of Independence and the Constitution of Philadelphia. Rothbard reads these events through the interpretive prism of radical libertarianism, unlike those historians who see the American Revolution as a conservative phenomenon (Rothbard, 1975, 2019). Rothbard also refers to Garet Garrett's "The Revolution Was," which discusses the imperialist drift of the United States and its abandonment of authentic American values (Garrett, 1953). Nor is there anything anti-Western about Rothbard, who shows a true reverence for Western culture, the Industrial Revolution, and the lifestyle and comforts typical of the West.

3 In Search of a Rational Foundation of Ethics

We have already discussed Rothbard's innovation in the Austrian school of economics—that he has taken to the extreme the classical liberal implications of a state limited in powers and functions and has theorized a society in which coercion is eliminated rather than merely limited to a minimum. He is not satisfied with and wants to go far beyond the nonavalutative defense of freedom and the free market typical of the Austrian school. His intent is to establish a foundation for an ethics that expresses what is good for man according to his own nature. He wishes to demonstrate that freedom and the free market are objective ethical values that are rationally based on the nature of man. To do this, he recovers the ancient tradition of natural law and its modern counterpart, introducing into the Austrian school a concept that was previously absent in it. This is ambitious and profoundly radical compared to the lessons of Mises. The existence of a system of norms that descend from the nature of man, that human reason is able to discover, and that precede the existence of the state and legal positivism is something potentially revolutionary that can pose a threat to the status quo—"a standing reproach to the reign of blindly traditional custom or the arbitrary will of the State apparatus" (Rothbard, 1998, p. 17).

This is how, in 1982, *The Ethics of Liberty* was born. Hans Hermann Hoppe, in his *Introduction* to the book, underlines the intertwining among the concept of private property right, free market economy, natural rights, history, and political philosophy, in the Rothbardian philosophical system (Hoppe, 1998, pp. xi–xliii). In this book, Rothbard again cites the sociologist Oppenheimer's distinction between the two different ways of acquiring wealth and obtaining income. One is that of voluntary production and exchange, the method of economic means; the other is that of the forced seizure of property, the method of political means. The nature of the human being, Rothbard tells us, is to live and prosper through production and exchange; therefore, those who live by the forced seizure of what belongs to others live against human nature and violate a universal ethics. But the state lives from the aggressive depredation of others—or taxation. Here is Rothbard's ethical reasoning briefly.

> Only the State obtains its revenue by coercion, by threatening dire penalties should the income not be forthcoming. That coercion is known as "taxation." … Taxation is theft, purely and simply, even though it is theft on a grand and colossal scale which no acknowledged criminals could hope to match. It is a compulsory seizure of the property of the State's inhabitants, or subjects … . Thus, the State is a coercive criminal organization that subsists by a regularized large-scale system of taxation-theft, and which gets away with it by engineering the support of the majority (*not,* again, of everyone) through securing an alliance with a group of opinion-moulding

> intellectuals whom it rewards with a share in its power and pelf (Rothbard, 1998, pp. 162, 172).

Indeed, Rothbard's interest in a rational foundation for an ethics of liberty arose many years earlier. We have already had occasion to quote the unpublished paper, written in 1954, "The Concept of 'Rational' and 'Irrational'," in which the criticism of Mises and political philosophy's claim to express value judgments about the ends of individuals appear for the first time (Rothbard, 1954, forthcoming). The topic of the rational foundation of ethics and the absolutism of values becomes predominant in Rothbard's commentary on the conference on relativism organized by the Volker Fund. The conference, held in 1960, featured a debate between Mises, Leoni, and Leo Strauss. Obviously, in this case, Rothbard sided with Strauss. In his prefatory note to "The Symposium on Relativism: A Critique," Rothbard specifies that he is in favor of the absolutism of values. "The absolutist believes that man's mind, employing reason ... is capable of discovering and knowing truth: including the truth about reality, and the truth about what is best for man and best for himself as an individual. The relativist denies this, denies that man's reason is capable of knowing truth, and does so by claiming that rather than being absolute, truth is relative to something else ... . Philosophically, I believe that libertarianism—and the wider creed of sound individualism of which libertarianism is a part—must rest on absolutism and deny relativism" (Rothbard, 2009, p. 104).

The Ethics of Liberty is based on the search for those eternal principles common to the whole human race that should be adhered to so that man can fully realize himself—so that he can prosper and live. This represents a clear and apparently definitive division within the Austrian school of economics, with Hayek and the Hayekians on one side and many of the American disciples of the school—Rothbard and the Rothbardians among them—on the other. Rothbard traces the differences within the Austrian School to the dichotomy between the Hayekian and Misesian paradigms—in particular, to the different attitudes of the two approaches toward human reason. Rothbard criticizes Hayek's emphasis on the discourse of unintended consequences that would, in reality, diminish the importance of intentional consequences or the rational projects of the individual. If, as Mises states, all human actions are aimed at an end, it would be much better, Rothbard argues, to make intentional and conscious what is only at the unintentional level (144–48). Rothbard criticizes the Hayekian theory of spontaneous order. In his opinion, it implies a lack of awareness on the part of the human being. Moreover, accepting such a theory would lead to a conservative and uncritical attitude toward those institutions that have simply grown spontaneously, including the state (Rothbard, 1997, pp. 144–148). Also useful for understanding the divisions among Austrians is an article by Joseph Salerno published in 1990. Salerno contrasts Mises's "rationalism" and Hayek's "irrational" emphasis on spontaneous order. Salerno's idea is that spontaneous and unintended consequences cannot be relied on to bring about social change (Salerno, 1990, pp. 50–51; see also Modugno, 2006, pp. 1279–1308). The concept of natural law is in some ways extraneous to the Austrian school of economics, which favors an evolutionary conception of institutions and law following the approach of Menger and Hayek. The criticism of Mises's report in "The Symposium on Relativism: A Critique," is paradigmatic. Rothbard distances himself from the praxeological and value-free defense of the free market that Mises proposes, and he instead supports the need for political philosophy to find universally valid basic values for life in society. Mises bases his own liberalism on the subjectivity of values and ends, but for Rothbard, this makes Mises "an ethical relativist … . Mises's utilitarian, relativist approach to ethics is not nearly enough to establish a full case for liberty. It must be supplemented by an absolutist ethics—an ethics of liberty, as well as of other values needed for the health and development of the individual— grounded on natural law, i.e., discovery of the laws of man's nature. Failure to recognize this is the greatest flaw in Mises's philosophical worldview" (Rothbard, 2009, pp. 111–112). The subjectivism of ends and values and the defense of the free market from a praxeological point of view are correct procedures in the context of praxeology, but they do not satisfy the Rothbardian need for ethics to have a rational basis. Praxeology, the science of human action, tells us that the free market economy is the best way of achieving the broadest possible well-being and the full range of human ends—ends that are subjective, as are the values that underlie them. Since economics deals with facts, it cannot have direct implications for ethics. For Mises, value judgments express merely subjective preferences, which cannot be considered true or false.

Rothbard disagrees with that view of ethics. His challenge is to show how one can convince others that the market economy—which is based on subjective values—is the best of all social systems. Mises believes that the free market is superior because of its results. Without denying that value judgments express subjective choices, he thinks that virtually everyone has good reason to support the free market. For Rothbard, certain facts about human nature give rise to objective judgments about what is best for man. He does not consider Mises's main arguments about capitalism to be fully sufficient. Mises's attempt to found capitalism on subjective grounds is valid but needs the support of another argument. Rothbard is among those authors who believe that, in practice, few of our judgments of facts are "pure" in the sense required by the fact-value dichotomy. Although, we cannot derive prescriptions from facts, we can derive them from judgments about facts. This is the position of Strauss (1950) and Foot (2001, 2002). Furthermore, Rothbard thinks there may be self-evident truths that can provide the basis for objective ethics, such as self-ownership of one's body. Mises, as is known, rejects this position because, for him, there are no criteria by which to objectively evaluate value judgments: "The ultimate goal of human action is always the satisfaction of the acting man's desire. There is no standard of greater or lesser satisfaction other than individual judgments of value, different for various people and for the same people at various times … . Nobody is in a position to decree what should make a fellow man happier" (Mises, 1998, p. 14). Given his ethical subjectivism, Mises rejects the whole notion of natural law. "But the teachings of utilitarian philosophy and classical economics have nothing at all to do with the doctrine of natural right … . They recommend popular government, private property, tolerance, and freedom not because they are natural and just, but because they are beneficial" (Mises, 1998, p. 174).

Why does Rothbard use an ethical argument to support the free market? He must have been aware that natural law was a very controversial subject. Mises's way of proceeding is correct in relation to praxeology, as Rothbard points out, but he is unable to tell us what is best for the human being. In short, Mises's speech does not adequately address the Rothbardian need to provide an objective and rational foundation for liberty. Mises shows that restrictive market economy policies have unintended consequences for most people. For this reason alone, he believes, everyone should accept the market economy. But Rothbard points out that the matter is not so simple. Some individuals may have a short-term interest in preferring heavily interventionist policies. They could be egalitarian to the point of preferring equal misery for all. Others could be nihilistic and want to bring about a scarcity of goods because they lament the excessive well-being of our society and its waste of resources. Still others may have a short-term interest in interventionist policies and want positions of power within the bureaucracy. Such possibilities counter

Mises's belief that all advocates of state interventionism would become supporters of the free market once they understood the logical consequences of a decline in market freedom. Rothbard's intention is to give greater persuasive force to Mises's arguments in support of freedom. Someone, according to Rothbard, who understands the benefits of a free market economy—welfare, peace, and cooperation—but opposes it, still faces an objective and rational ethical argument. Rothbard finds in natural law a guide for discerning which ends are better for man—that is, which ends align with human nature, understood as the drive to live and prosper. "The natural law, then, elucidates what is best for man—what ends man should pursue that are most harmonious with, and best tend to fulfill, his nature" (Rothbard, 1998, p. 12).

The Aristotelian-Thomist approach to the idea of natural law plays a very important role in Rothbard's theory, which takes up the idea of an order of natural laws that can be discovered by reason. "In the Thomistic tradition, natural law is ethical as well as physical law; and the instrument by which man apprehends such law is his *reason* .... Aquinas, then, realized that men always act purposively, but also went beyond this to argue that ends can also be apprehended by reason as either objectively good or bad for man" (Rothbard, 1998, pp. 6–7). Rothbard attributes the same reproach of ethical relativism to Bruno Leoni, because "he is scornful of the very idea that ethical values should be rationally demonstrated," while "values should be demonstrated because reason is the only sure, solid ground of conviction about values" (Rothbard, 2009, p. 106). Rothbard, unlike Mises, thought that ethical principles could be deduced from certain facts about human nature. "Individual human beings are not born or fashioned with fully formed knowledge, values, goals, or personalities; they must each form their own values and goals, develop their personalities, and learn about themselves and the world around them. Every man must have freedom, must have the scope to form, test, and act upon his own choices, for any sort of development of his own personality to take place. He must, in short, be free in order that he may be fully human" (Rothbard, 1997, pp. 3–4). Rothbard's approach seems very close to the so-called Veatch school because it is characterized by the recovery of Aristotelian-Thomist metaphysics for the foundation of natural law and the consequent anchoring of natural rights Veatch (1962, 1971). Even when Rothbard adopts an axiomatic-deductive approach, beginning with the axiom of human action—considered a self-evident truth—he situates this axiom within an Aristotelian-Thomist framework, grounding it in human nature rather than in the logical structure of the human mind, as a Kantian approach would Rothbard (1957). Rothbard, on the other hand, derives the right of self-ownership from natural law rather than taking it as an axiom. Self-ownership is in tune with what he supposes to be the natural end of the human being—namely, the promotion of his own survival.

Concerning the Straussian conception, Rothbard questions the thesis that identifies the modern theory of natural rights as a break with the past. He places more emphasis on continuity with the past rather than sharp division, and according to the continuity thesis, individual natural rights derive from natural law. Rothbard underlines the Scholastic, Thomist, and Christian roots of the Lockean doctrine of natural rights. In the individualism of modern natural rights theory, Rothbard finds not a corruption but an enrichment of the natural law tradition, as well as the beginning of a new way to understand human means and political ends. Thus, while Rothbard appreciates the Straussian idea of natural law as a battle against the prevailing relativism of values, he is unable to accept Strauss's invitation to reclaim "the classic natural right doctrine in its original form" that, "if fully developed, is identical with the doctrine of the best regime" (Strauss, 1950, p. 144). In support of a link between Thomism and the Grotian development of natural law, Rothbard quotes Alessandro Passerin d'Entrèves: the "definition of natural law has nothing revolutionary. When he maintains that natural law is that body of rules which man is able to discover by the use of his reason, he does nothing but restate the Scholastic notion of a rational foundation of ethics. Indeed, his aim is rather to restore that notion which had been shaken by the extreme Augustinianism of certain Protestant currents of thought. When he declares that these rules are valid in themselves, independently of the fact that God willed them, he repeats an assertion which had already been made by some of the Schoolmen." The aim of Grotius "was to construct a system of laws which would carry conviction in an age in which theological controversy was gradually losing the power to do so" (Rothbard, 1998, p. 5; Passerin d'Entreves, 1954, pp. 51–52). It has been pointed out that the continuity between natural law and natural rights in the thought of d'Entrèves probably refers more to the function historically carried out by natural law rather than to a doctrinal continuity (Cubeddu, 2004, pp. 179–210). In turn, Rothbard adds that "Grotius and his juristic successors—Pufendorf, Burlamaqui, and Vattel—proceeded to elaborate this independent body of natural laws in a purely secular context, in accordance with their own particular interests, which were not, in contrast to the Schoolmen, primarily theological. Indeed, even the eighteenth-century rationalists, in many ways dedicated enemies of the Scholastics, were profoundly influenced in their very rationalism by the Scholastic tradition" (Rothbard, 1998, p. 6). Elsewhere, Rothbard points out that

> the scholastics may have dominated medieval and post-medieval traditions, but that despite this fact, they were pioneers and elaborators of the natural law *and* natural rights traditions. The pitting of "tradition" vs "modernity" is largely an artificial antithesis … . Locke may have been and indeed was an ardent Protestant, but he was also a Protestant scholastic, heavily influenced by the founder of Protestant scholasticism, the Dutchman Hugo Grotius, who in turn was heavily influenced by the late Spanish Catholic scholastics … . While Locke developed libertarian natural rights thought more fully than his predecessors, it was still squarely embedded in the scholastic natural law tradition (Rothbard, 1995a, Vol 1; 1995b, Vol 2, pp. 313–314)

Within this framework, Rothbard's conception of the connection between natural law and natural rights becomes more nuanced as he highlights the contributions of the Levellers and Locke, particularly in advancing the idea of individualism. If the Aristotelian vision of man led to the idea that the state is the place of good and virtuous action, "it was, in contrast, the Levellers and particularly John Locke in seventeenth-century England who transformed classical natural law into a theory grounded on methodological and hence political individualism" (Rothbard, 1998, p. 21). The continuity thesis has been supported by the work of Brian Tierney, whose research decisively challenges the notion of a sharp opposition between the ancient Aristotelian doctrine of natural law and the modern theory of subjective individual rights (Tierney, 1997). The Rothbardian position, however, is particularly original both for its deduction of the axiom of nonaggression from the right of self-ownership—the true cornerstone of the Rothbardian system, which integrates the classic triad of the natural rights to life, liberty, and property—and for the extreme consequences that Rothbard sees in the nature and role of the state. Rothbard wants "to establish an objective ethics which affirms the overriding value of liberty, and morally condemns all forms of statism" (Rothbard, 1998, p. 214).

3.1 Secession

Secessionism is a central theme not only in libertarian reflection but also in classical liberalism. The American colonists seceded from the mother country on the basis of the Lockean principle—contained in the Declaration of Independence—according to which if a government violates the rights that it is supposed to protect, then individuals have the right to abandon that government. Moreover, Mises himself, in a famous passage about secession, writes the following:

> The right of self-determination in regard to the question of membership in a state thus means: whenever the inhabitants of a particular territory, whether it be a single village, a whole district, or a series of adjacent districts, make it known, by a freely conducted plebiscite, that they no longer wish to remain united to the state to which they belong at the time, but wish either to form an independent state or to attach themselves to some other state, their wishes are to be respected and complied with. This is the only feasible and effective way of preventing revolutions and civil and international wars ... . However, the right of self-determination of which we speak is not the right of self-determination of nations, but rather the right of self-determination of the inhabitants of every territory large enough to form an independent administrative unit. If it were in any way possible to grant this right of self-determination to every individual person, it would have to be done (Mises, 2005, pp. 79–80).

Here, it can be seen why Mises is a source of inspiration for radical and rationalist positions. For Rothbard, the right to secession is based on the natural rights of individuals. He hypothesizes the possibility of a secession of a single region, a city, a neighborhood, a street, an apartment building—all the way down to the individual. Just as a person has every right to turn to another company for a particular service, so too he should be able to choose the agency for his police protection and administration of justice. Rothbard has addressed the theme of secession several times, but "Nations by Consent: Decomposing the Nation-State," (Rothbard, 1994), an article published in the *Journal of Libertarian Studies*, is particularly significant, marking a turning point and a new awareness on the part not only of Rothbard but of libertarians in general. The essay comes out of that period, following the fall of the Berlin Wall, in which libertarians led by Rothbard and Rockwell saw a propitious opportunity for the rebirth of something very similar to the Old Right: a paleolibertarian movement, which was liberal in economics, noninterventionist in foreign policy, and conservative in its commitment to traditional values.

> With the implosion of the communist regimes and the Soviet Union, Rothbard witnessed the decomposition of the centralized state in Eastern Europe and the emergence of authentic nations. In fact, Rothbard specifies, taking up Mises and Nock, the nation is something different from the state. The nation, and not the nation state, is that cultural community characterized by a context of history, language, values, and traditions within which the individual is born and for whom all these aspects are fundamental for his identity as a human being. The modern nation state was born with the violent conquest of other peripheral nationalities but often without succeeding in subduing and uprooting the authentic local cultural identities, as in the case of Scotland, Catalonia, Bretons, Basques, and Languedoc. "If we proceed with the decomposition and decentralization of the modern centralizing and coercive nation-state, deconstructing that state into constituent nationalities and neighborhoods, we shall at one and the same time reduce the scope of government power, the scope, and importance of voting and the extent of social conflict. The scope of private contract, and of voluntary consent, will be enhanced, and the brutal and repressive state will be gradually dissolved into a harmonious and increasingly prosperous social order" (Rothbard, 1994, pp. 17–18). This means rethinking secessionist movements, which take on a deep meaning in this context and should be supported and encouraged by libertarians around the world.

This important essay by Rothbard, which also represents his cultural legacy, marks a rethinking of open borders and total migratory freedom. In fact, a libertarian society based on the anarchocapitalist model could not function with these features. In a society where everything is private—where every territory or neighborhood is private—immigration would be regulated by the owners. There would be communities closed to immigration and ethnically homogeneous, and others would be ethnically open. Some communities would allow prostitution, pornography, and abortion, while others would prohibit them. In the essay, Rothbard declares that he has rethought indiscriminate immigration after observing the great problems that it creates in terms of both the welfare state, which weighs heavily on citizens' taxes, and cultural invasion, which in some cases destroys local culture. Ultimately the open border system is a decision imposed by the central government, often against the wishes of the owners.

References

Arendt, H. (1951). *The origins of totalitarianism*. Schocken Books.

Bassani, L. M. (2011). Introduzione in J. Calhoun, *Disquisizione sul potere*. Liberilibri.

Beito, D. T. (2002). The mutual aid tradition of American fraternal societies before the twentieth century. In D. T. Beito, P. Gordon, & A. Tabarrok (Eds.), *Voluntary city: Choice, community, and civil society*. Independent Institute.

Block, W. (2018). *Defending the undefendable*. Ludwig von Mises Institute, Original work published 1976.

Block, W. (2021). Murray Rothbard, anarchist. *Studia Z Historii Filosofi*, *12*, 4.

Bodin, J. (1992). *On Sovereignty: Four chapters from the six books of the commonwealth* (Edited and translated by Julian H. Franklin). Cambridge University Press. Original work published 1576.

Botero, G. (2017). *The Reason of State* (Edited and translated by Robert Bireley). Cambridge University Press. Original work published 1589.

Bourne, R. (1998). *The state*. See Sharp.

Brunner, O. (1939). *Land und Herrschaft: Grundfragen der territorialen Verfassungsgeschichte Südostdeutschlands im Mittelalter*. Rohrer.

Cubeddu, R. (2004). La concezione del diritto naturale. S. Noto (Ed.), *Alessandro Passerin d'Entrèves pensatore europeo*. Il Mulino.

de Jasay, A. (1985). *The state*. Liberty Fund.

Foot, P. (2001). *Natural goodness*. Clarendon Press.

Foot, P. (2002). *Virtues and vices*. Oxford University Press.

Garrett, G. (1953). The revolution was. In *The people's pottage*. Caxton.

Green, D. G. (2002). Medical care through mutual aid: The friendly societies of Great Britain. In D. T. Beito, P. Gordon, & A. Tabarrok (Eds.), *Voluntary city*.

Hayek, F. (1949). The intellectuals and socialism. *University of Chicago Law Review*.

Hayek, F. V. (2021). *Law, legislation and liberty*. University of Chicago Press, Original work published 1973–1979.

Hobbes, T. (2012) *Leviathan*. N. Malcolm (Ed.). Clarendon Press. Original work published 1651.

Hoppe, H. H. (1998) Introduction to M. N. Rothbard, *The Ethics of Liberty*. New York University Press.

Keynes, J. M. (1927). *The End of Laissez-Faire*. L. & Virginia Woolf.

Keynes, J. M. (1936). *The general theory of employment, interest and money*. Harcourt Brace.

La Boétie, É. D. (1975). *The politics of obedience: The discourse on voluntary servitude*. Black Rose Books, Original work published 1576.

Latouche, S. (2007). *Petit traité de la décroissance sereine*. Hachette.

Machiavelli, N. (1961). *The Prince*. Penguin. Original work published 1513.
McElroy, W. (1991). *Freedom, feminism and the state: An overview of individualist feminism*. Independent Institute.
Mill, J. S. (1991). *On liberty*. Routledge, Original work published 1859.
Mises, L. V. (1998). *Human action: A treatise on economics*. Ludwig von Mises Institute, Original work published 1949.
Mises, L. V. (2005). *Liberalism: The classical tradition*. Liberty Fund, Original work published 1927.
Modugno, R. (2009). (Ed.). *Rothbard versus the philosophers: Unpublished writings on Hayek, Mises, Strauss, and Polanyi*. Ludwig von Mises Institute.
Modugno, R. A. (2006). Un dialogue entre les Autrichiens et les libertariens américain. In P. Nemo & J. Petitot (Eds.), *Histoire du libéralisme en Europe*. Presses Universitaires de France.
Montesquieu, C. L. D. S. (1977). *The Spirit of Laws*. University of California Press, Original work published 1748.
Napolitano, A. (2019). Constitutional Chaos in America. *The Austrian*, 4–5.
Norberg, J. (2016). *Progress: Ten reasons to look forward to the future*. Oneworld.
Passerin D' Entrèves, A. (1954). *La dottrina del diritto naturale*. Edizioni di Comunità.
Paterson, I. (1996). *The god of the machine*. Transaction, Original work published 1943.
Rawls, J. (1971). *A theory of justice*. Belknap Press of Harvard University Press.
Rothbard, M. N. (Forthcoming). The concepts 'rational' and 'irrational,' March 1954. In R. A.Modugno (Ed.), *Murray Rothbard on politics, philosophy, and history: A selection from his papers*. Ludwig von Mises Institute.
Rothbard, M. N. (1957). In defense of 'Extreme Apriorism'. *Southern Economic Journal*, *23*(3), 314–320.
Rothbard, M. N. (1973). *For a new liberty: The libertarian manifesto*. Macmillan.
Rothbard, M. N. (1975). *Conceived in liberty*, Vol. 4.
Rothbard, M. N. (1994). Nations by consent: Decomposing the nation-state. *Journal of Libertarian Studies*, *11*(1), 1–10.
Rothbard, M. N. (1995a). An Austrian perspective on the history of economic thought. In *Economic thought before adam smith*, (Vol. 1). Edward Elgar.
Rothbard, M. N. (1995b). *An Austrian perspective on the history of economic thought*. In *Classical Economics* (Vol. 2). Edward Elgar.
Rothbard, M. N. (1997). *The logic of action one: Method, money and the Austrian school*. Edward Elgar.
Rothbard, M. N. (1998). *The ethics of liberty*. New York University Press, Original work published 1982.
Rothbard, M. N. (2000). Conservation in the free market. In *egalitarianism as a revolt against nature and other essays*. Ludwig von Mises Institute, Original work published 1970.

Rothbard, M. N. (2019). Conceived in liberty. In P. Newman (Ed.), *A New Republic* (Vol. 5). Ludwig von Mises Institute.

Rothbard, M. N. (Forthcoming). Rothbard to F. A. Harper, January 3, 1961. In R. A. Modugno (Ed.) *Murray Rothbard on politics, philosophy, and history: A selection from his papers*. Ludwig von Mises Institute.

Salerno, J. T. (1990). Ludwig von Mises as social rationalist. *Review of Austrian Economics*, *4*, 26–54.

Strauss, L. (1950). *Natural right and history*. University of Chicago Press.

Thornton, M. (1991). *The economics of prohibition*. University of Utah Press.

Tierney, B. (1997). *The idea of natural rights: Studies on natural rights, natural law, and church law 1150–1625*. Scholars Press.

Veatch, H. (1962). *Rational man: A modern interpretation of aristotelian ethics*. University of Indiana Press.

Veatch, H. (1971). *For an ontology of morals: A critique of contemporary ethical theory*. Northwestern University Press.

CHAPTER 5

Legacy

Keywords Mises institute · paleolibertarianism · populism · Italy · Spain · France · Argentina

1 Murray N. Rothbard's Successors

Rothbard was an extremely prolific and active author, managing to make libertarianism an autonomous current of thought and a movement with specific characteristics. In a very original way, he managed to combine Austrian economics, an ethics based on natural rights, the American individualist-anarchist tradition, and a great passion for the history of economic thought, explaining all the while, through an elaboration of the anti-statist legacy, how and why the government oppresses and robs the majority of the population. From an institutional point of view, he helped to found or otherwise worked with the major libertarian organizations from the 1940s to the 1990s, including the Foundation for Economic Education, the Volker Fund, the Institute for Humane Studies, the Libertarian Party, the Cato Institute, and the Ludwig von Mises Institute—the dream of a lifetime. Through his commitment, he has contributed to the formation of new generations of Austrian economists and libertarians in the United States and internationally.

R. A. Modugno, *The Legacy of Murray N. Rothbard*, Palgrave Studies in Austrian Economics,
https://doi.org/10.1007/978-3-032-06870-5_5

He has influenced scholars whose works are now considered classics of libertarian literature. In Walter Block's *Defending the Undefendable*, which was strongly influenced by Rothbard, the author defends all those actions and behaviors that, although considered morally reprehensible, do not involve victims—that is, that resolve in free negotiations between consenting adults. Here, the prostitute, the ruffian, the drug dealer, the drug addict, the corrupt policeman, the forger, and the usurer become members of society who cannot be prosecuted. In the words of Lysander Spooner, vices are not crimes (Spooner, 2020). With the evolution of the libertarian movement—and the maturation of Rothbard's own thought—giving rise to paleolibertarianism, Block added an afterword to the most recent edition of *Defending the Undefendable*—eloquently titled "Mea Culpa"—in which he admits that the first edition (1976) betrayed a certain sympathetic attitude toward immoral but legitimate behavior. He also writes that he was influenced by a certain libertine climate in the 1970s, but that with maturity, marriage, family, and religion, even while not denying that vices are not crimes if they do not involve victims, he cannot approve of certain behaviors (Block, 2018). This has been the path of the whole libertarian movement of the Rothbardian matrix. Even if certain actions are not punishable by law, they may still be considered reprehensible. Paleolibertarianism detaches itself from any possible overlap with libertine attitudes. In fact, it defends the bourgeois elements that built the West: its work ethic, Industrial Revolution, and middle class, which has been harassed by an increasingly predatory state, by the bureaucracy of the welfare state, and by the oppression of public schools. Paleolibertarianism also avoids any temptation that, taken to its extreme consequences, coincides with egalitarianism and collectivism, substituting one elite for another. The antiestablishment attitude leads, in fact, to a specific and noble kind of populism—what Rothbard called a right-wing populism, which is nothing more than the recognition that the majority of the population, including a hard-working middle class, is ruled and oppressed by elites—a coalition of big government, big business, bureaucracy, and politicians allied with and dominated by big corporations, financial elites, intellectuals, and the opinion-molding class (Rothbard, 1992, p. 7). We need to remember that Rothbard didn't defend populism uncritically, as Gordon puts it, "he saw danger in leftist populism; a true populist movement must not abandon the free market in favor of crackpot panaceas" (Gordon, 2007, p. 108).

One of Rothbard's more well-known followers is Hans-Hermann Hoppe, a philosopher and social theorist who developed a new defense of Rothbard's libertarian political philosophy, which he based on what he called argumentation ethics. Hoppe interpreted the question of how areas within national territories should be managed in the absence of privatization. When an area is either unowned or treated as a form of collective private property by its residents, who is responsible for paying taxes? According to Hoppe's argument, the free circulation of goods and capital can never violate anyone's rights, since it is always the result of an exchange, but the free movement of persons is different. The immigrant can violate the private property of others if no one has consented to his immigration. If there is no consent, then there is no voluntary relationship between the parties. For Hoppe, therefore, the most consistent libertarian principle here is the freedom to welcome but also the right to exclude. According to Hoppe's paleolibertarianism, the immigration issue cannot be solved centrally, because it can never account for everyone's needs. It should instead be resolved at the most decentralized and local level possible—country, city, neighborhood, ward, or street—as in those authentic realities of applied libertarianism that are the American gated communities—Rothbardian private cities organized on the model of the condominium (McKenzie, 1994; Beito et al., 2001).

The text by Hoppe that has caused the most sensation is *Democracy: The God That Failed*, which has the merit of taking to their logical conclusion Rothbard's own, but also Hayek's, criticisms and perplexities concerning democracy (Hoppe, 2001). In this book, the author submits to corrosive criticism what is considered one of the greatest achievements of humanity: democracy. On the basis of historical analysis and economic reasoning, Hoppe first considers the transition from monarchy to democracy as a process of decay rather than progress. A monarch will always have a long-term perspective on the management of the assets and resources of his kingdom, while the democratic representative, who has only been elected for a certain period of time, will always have a short-term, hit-and-run vision and will try to exploit his temporary position of power and the resources available to him as quickly as possible instead of safeguarding and enhancing them for the future. Of course, this does not mean that Hoppe admires the monarchy. His ideal is small, self-governing communities. Self-government is possible only in small communities, and freedom and private property are incompatible with democracy, which aims at egalitarianism and income redistribution, inevitably violating the right to private property.

Among Rothbard's most important successors is Joseph Salerno, the foremost economist continuing Rothbard's work in Austrian economics.

Salerno is especially well-known for his work in money and banking, including a history of the dispute between the banking and currency schools in nineteenth-century Britain. He has also done important work on Ludwig von Mises, such as his account of Mises as a social rationalist and his differentiation of Mises's calculation argument against socialism from the knowledge-based approach of F. A. Hayek. His book *Money: Sound and Unsound* applies the Austrian monetary theory to historical and contemporary events, examines the role of the Federal Reserve System, and discusses the necessity of protecting money from the destructive influence of the state (Salerno, 2010). Here, we should also mention David Gordon, who was praised by Rothbard for his extensive knowledge in many different fields. He is mainly known as a book reviewer, and he is especially interested in analytic philosophy.

Rothbard's tireless work, including through the Ludwig von Mises Institute, has had an influence far beyond the borders of the United States and has involved young and old from Latin America and Western and Eastern Europe. In Italy, Rothbard's influence has extended beyond economics to fields such as political philosophy, philosophy of law, and the history of political thought, giving rise to editorial initiatives from publishers such as Rubbettino Editore, Liberilibri, and IBL Libri, the imprint of the think tank Istituto Bruno Leoni. Several scholars, including Raimondo Cubeddu, Sergio Ricossa, and Enrico Colombatto, have worked, and continue to work, on libertarian themes. Many of them, including Marco Bassani, Carlo Lottieri, and Alberto Mingardi, stand alongside the freedom movements in Venezuela and the secessionist movements.

Rothbard's influence has spread to Spain as well, and here the work of the economist Jesús Huerta de Soto is of particular significance. His lectures on Austrian economics are notable for their clarity and historical erudition, and his extensive research on the history of banking supports Rothbard's position that fractional reserve banking is fraudulent.

There are important scholars influenced by Rothbard in France, too—in particular, Jacques Garello and Pascal Salin. The first, in 1989, founded the Institute for Economic Studies–Europe, which gathered many young students to teach them Rothbardian and Austrian principles. Pascal Salin, in his *Tax Tyranny*, shows a clear Rothbardian influence (Salin, 2020). In 2023, Javier Milei was elected president in Argentina. Milei is the first head of state to openly and consistently declare himself an anarchocapitalist and to consider the state an enemy (Bagus, 2025, p. 215). The theoretical corpus that inspires and supports his government policy is a radical libertarianism firmly anchored in the tradition of the Austrian school of economics and its cardinal principles, including human action as a foundational axiom, the use of the deductive and a priori method as an epistemological basis, and methodological subjectivism as an interpretative criterion of economic phenomena. A decisive experience for Milei was his reading of a chapter of *Man, Economy, and State*. This marked a radical intellectual turning point for him, so much so that he questioned 25 years of study and academic activity and was led to an intransigent intellectual militancy in support of anarchocapitalism (Bagus, 2025, pp. 174–176). Milei condemns socialism because of the impossibility of economic calculation in the absence of market prices and because of the structural contradictions inherent in any form of state interventionism. He also addresses current issues such as climate change and the scarcity of resources through a strictly libertarian perspective (Bagus, 2025, pp. 195–196, 203–207). Argentina, the country Milei inherited, was socially, economically, and culturally devastated, its political system delegitimized, and its currency in deep crisis. At the time of Milei's inauguration, the country was on the verge of hyperinflation. All this was because of decades of Peronist interventionism. But since the new president's inauguration, Argentina has emerged from recession after six months of continuous growth.

References

Bagus, P. (2025). *La era Milei: El despertar libertario*. Preface by Javier Milei. Orden Espontáneo.

Beito, D. T., Gordon, P., & Tabarrok, A. (Eds.). (2001). *The voluntary city: Choice, community, and civil society*. Independent Institute.

Block, W. (2018). *Defending the undefendable*. Ludwig von Mises Institute, Original work published 1976.

Gordon, D. (2007). *The Essential Rothbard*. Ludwig von Mises Institute.

Hoppe, H. H. (2001). *Democracy: The god that failed*. Transaction.

McKenzie, E. (1994). *Privatopia*. Yale University Press.

Rothbard, M. N. (1992). *Right-Wing Populism: A Strategy for the Paleo Movement*. Rothbard–Rockwell Report.

Salerno, J. T. (2010). *Money: Sound and Unsound*. Ludwig von Mises Institute.

Salin, P. (2020). *Tax Tyrrany*. Edward Elgar.

Spooner, L. (2020). *Vices are not crimes*. Ludwig von Mises Institute, Original work published 1875.

Conclusion

In conclusion, the paleolibertarian legacy of preferring small-scale political structures leads Rothbard's heirs to look favorably on localist and secessionist movements and to regard with absolute distrust any form of supranational Leviathan. Murray Rothbard, Llewellyn Rockwell, Joseph T. Salerno, David Gordon, Jeff Deist, Hans-Hermann Hoppe, and Ralph Raico, on the cultural side, and Ron Paul and Rand Paul, on the political side, have been proposing a "paleo" turn since the early 90's. The purpose of this turning point was ideally to reconnect to the roots of the Old Right—the American anti-Roosevelt Right—what had been Rothbard's starting point: reinvigorating noninterventionism in foreign policy in the post–Cold War era, protecting local communities from the centralizing claims of the federal government and other supranational institutions, and affirming the importance of the cultural battle in defense of values—traditional Western values, the only ones we own. It is therefore of fundamental importance to defend the Western cultural heritage from multiculturalism, political correctness, wokeism, and inclusiveness; to contest the proliferation of state privileges granted to any group officially designated as an "oppressed minority"; to recognize the important role played by the Christian religion, and particularly of Catholic philosophy, in the moral foundations of our civilization; and to emphasize the close connection between the institutions of a libertarian society—the market, property rights, individual freedoms, and the traditional and bourgeois cultural values underlying them—and defend these against the expansion of statism and welfarism.

R. A. Modugno, *The Legacy of Murray N. Rothbard*, Palgrave Studies in Austrian Economics,
https://doi.org/10.1007/978-3-032-06870-5

Index

R. A. Modugno, *The Legacy of Murray N. Rothbard*, Palgrave Studies in Austrian Economics,
https://doi.org/10.1007/978-3-032-06870-5